ECONOMIC ANALYSIS OF ENVIRONMENTAL POLICIES

D.N. Dewees, C.K. Everson, and W.A. Sims

Economic Analysis of Environmental Policies

PUBLISHED FOR THE ONTARIO ECONOMIC COUNCIL BY
UNIVERSITY OF TORONTO PRESS
TORONTO AND BUFFALO

© Ontario Economic Council 1975
Printed in Canada
ISBN 0-8020-3335-0
LC 75-37171

Contents

Preface

This monograph was prepared at the request, and under the sponsorship, of the Ontario Economic Council. Grant Reuber, the chairman of the council, wished to gather together some of the generally accepted economic wisdom on environmental policy, and relate it, where possible, to the current Ontario situation. The result was to be aimed at those with at least an undergraduate training in economics: government economists, graduate economists, third- or fourth-year undergraduate economics students. Whatever the merits of reaching a wider audience, it was felt that too much space would be required to do so and still cover the desired topics.

As the reader will discover, this monograph does not treat all areas of the subject. Many important tools, such as linear programming and input-output analysis, have been omitted. Sophisticated feedback policies involving ambient monitoring and source regulation are only touched upon in one case study. The vast body of water quality management literature is only briefly alluded to. The omitted topics are not unimportant; there was simply no time for them. We hope the topics that are covered are carefully analysed and presented.

Limited as this work is, it could not have been completed in one year without substantial previous experience and research. I am indebted to the Inland Waters Branch of the Canadian Department of the Environment for supporting my water management research with a five-year development grant to the Institute of Environmental Sciences and Engineering of the University of Toronto (now the Institute for Environmental Studies). A graduate course in environmental economics, supported by the Institute for Environmental Studies, produced some of the ideas in this monograph. The Institute for Policy Analysis (also of the University of Toronto) has provided an atmosphere conducive to thinking about policy questions. The Department of Political Economy has supported an undergraduate course in environmental economics that has been the source of many stimulating ideas and discussions. Discussions with colleagues, particularly John Dales, and with both graduate and undergraduate students have all contributed to the formulation of the framework for analysis presented here.

The attribution of chapters to joint authors is not easy in this case since all three of us worked on each. Primary authorship, however, was as follows: Dewees, chapters 1, 2, 5, and 6 and the third section of chapter 7; Everson, chapter 3 and the first and second sections of chapter 7; Sims, chapter 4 and the first and second sections of chapter 7. Several rounds of debate, discussions, and editing mean that to some extent we are all responsible for the whole. The authors are listed in alphabetical order because it would be impossible to derive a ranking based on effort.

DND

Abbreviations

acfm	actual cubic feet per minute
ALAD	aminolevulinic acid dehydrase
BOD	biochemical oxygen demand
Cl	chlorine
Cl$^-$	chlorides
COD	chemical oxygen demand
DO	dissolved oxygen
INCO	International Nickel Company of Canada
kwh	kilowatt hour
mgd	million gallons per day
μg/g	micrograms per gram
μg/100 ml	micrograms per hundred millilitres
μg/m^3	micrograms per cubic metre
MW	megawatts
PCA	pollution control authority
ppm	parts per million
scfm	standard cubic feet per minute
SO$_3$	sulphite
TVA	Tennessee Valley Authority

ECONOMIC ANALYSIS OF ENVIRONMENTAL POLICIES

1
Introduction

It is sometimes suggested that pollution should be eliminated by absolute prohibitions against any discharge of waste into the air or water. As a practical matter, however, it is often impossible to achieve zero discharge. We do not have the technology for 100 per cent removal of many pollutants from stack gases and discharge water. Thus the total prohibition of emissions would eliminate the production of many goods, necessities as well as luxuries. Furthermore, some pollutants have a lower threshold level below which they are not perceptible or not harmful or both. It would be hard to justify expenditures to reduce pollution when it is not harmful or when it cannot be distinguished from naturally occurring background levels of the pollutant.

The question is thus not whether to allow pollution but how much pollution to allow. In a society that must satisfy its needs from limited resources we must decide how to allocate these resources among many competing needs. No single goal, such as pollution control, can command unlimited quantities of these resources.

For many years most economic analysis concentrated on situations in which it could be assumed that markets operated reasonably efficiently in allocating resources among competing users. During the last decade or so, however, there has been increasing recognition that important problems lie in areas where markets do not operate efficiently. One such area, labelled 'technological external diseconomies,' includes most pollution or environmental problems. By now a substantial literature has emerged developing theories that can be applied to environmental problems and undertaking empirical analysis of actual or simulated environmental problems. In short, there now exists a body of literature that can be entitled 'environmental economics.'

The economic analysis of environmental problems is strongly rooted in several long-established areas of economic theory. The behaviour of large numbers of polluters and pollutees can be explained by the theory of externalities, recognizing interactions between economic units without a market transaction. The same behaviour can also be analysed as a problem in information and transaction costs, since a world of perfect and costless information could lead to bargaining by individuals or groups to internalize the externality. Cost-benefit analysis and cost-effectiveness analysis are frequently used to evaluate pollution control projects. The literature on public goods and their supply can be used in evaluation of policies designed to improve environmental quality, or to allocate more efficiently this scarce resource. Most analytical tools of the environmental economist can be found in, or derived from, the applied economist's bag of tools, including input-output analysis, macroeconomic modelling, cost-benefit analysis, multivariate regression analysis, linear programming, and other maximization or minimization techniques. But environmental economics is distinguished from other established economic fields by different assumptions and interdisciplinary influences.

This monograph reviews the literature of environmental economics, expands it in places, and relates it to environmental policy problems in Ontario. The ways in which such problems have been analysed in the past are reviewed and new methods suggested. Lines of research that might contribute to better policy-making in the future are also indicated.

The theoretical analysis presented should be equally applicable to any situation in which, although there is no market transaction, economic activity causes undesirable effects on other individuals or firms by direct physical interaction. The case studies and empirical analysis, however, will concentrate upon air and water pollution problems. These two areas are selected because they are the subject of the bulk of past empirical research. Furthermore, the methodology applied here will in general be applicable to other forms of pollution, such as noise pollution, aesthetic degradation, and solid waste problems, detailed treatment of which would only increase the size of this monograph without substantially broadening its analytical content.

The second chapter presents a framework for economic analysis of environmental problems. It surveys the literature on the theory of externalities as an explanation for the existence and persistence of environmental problems. A set of objectives for environmental policy is presented and evaluated. We then consider how to determine what amount of pollution control is desirable, and who should bear the cost of that control. Finally, we examine the view that, since all economic activity is interrelated, environmental problems should be considered simultaneously rather than in isolation.

The third chapter examines the benefits of pollution control. The theoretical tools and analytical methods for estimating benefits are considered and criticized. The best available empirical studies are summarized and their results presented. The few studies of pollution control benefits in Ontario are given particular attention, because they indicate the best available evidence for Ontario and suggest what kind of data would be available for future studies in this provinces. These benefit estimates are critical for determining desired levels of pollution control, and even for choosing between alternative kinds of regulatory policy.

The fourth chapter considers the cost of air and water pollution control. The best available methodologies for estimating control costs are presented and discussed, and some suggestions are made for improving them. Empirical results are also summarized, again with special attention to Ontario, and suggestions are made for future research. This cost information is important for determining how much pollution control to require and who should bear the burden of pollution control, and for deciding the cost impact of alternative control policies.

The fifth chapter explores the cost of information and monitoring for pollution control and the impact of these costs on control policies. Current programs for monitoring ambient air and water quality and pollution emissions are reviewed, with special emphasis on Ontario practices. The costs of these monitoring programs are considered as well as the cost and effectiveness of different degrees and types of monitoring. We consider the information needs of alternative control policies and the impact of any difference found here on the choice of policy for a particular problem. Although economists have tended to ignore measurement and information costs, it is clear that in practice these may be decisive factors in choice of policy and in the effectiveness of many programs.

The sixth chapter analyses alternative administrative arrangements for controlling emissions. The regulatory standard, the effluent charge, and the pollution rights system are described and compared in terms of the objective set forth in the second chapter. Their costs and effectiveness are also considered. Other parameters of environmental policy are discussed, including local variations in standards or goals, the role of environmental quality standards in pollution control, and problems of timing of policies.

Finally in the seventh chapter we consider several case studies of environmental problems in Ontario and actual or hypothetical policy approaches. The nature of the problem, the data available, and the probable consequences of alternative policies are discussed. A policy that seems best suited to the problem is recommended, based upon the analysis in the preceding chapters. These case studies provide an example of how the analysis can be brought to bear on particular problems to yield reasonable policy recommendations.

It is hoped that this monograph will indicate the current state of the art in economic analysis of environmental problems. It is not our purpose to offer final solutions to environmental problems generally or to specific Ontario problems. While general forms for satisfactory solutions will be suggested, environmental problems present administrative and technological variations. For years economists have recommended effluent charges as the solution to pollution problems. This almost unanimous and continuous advice has been virtually ignored in solving important policy problems, in part because it is too general. Such general advice is worthless for drafting legislation, and economists have rarely advanced from this advice to suggest specific policies capable of being written into law. Nor will we. A particular problem requires a solution designed specifically for that problem, and presenting specific solutions is beyond the scope of this monograph. We can only hope to show how such solutions should be pursued, and how they may be evaluated.

We thus present some ideas, some tools, and some results that should be useful to policy-makers for the analysis and solution of environmental problems. We also indicate where current theory or empirical understanding is particularly weak and therefore not strongly supportive of policy recommendations. We shall attempt to indicate where further research might be particularly productive in improving environmental policies. Unfortunately, the most productive research may not be on the most important problems, simply because it is apparent that some of them, because of empirical or theoretical limitations, cannot possibly yield to even a major research effort for many years.

Finally, we emphasize the relative modesty of this work. The theoretical economic literature on environmental problems is already large and growing rapidly. In addition, an enormous amount of empirical research on costs and benefits, performed by economists, engineers, doctors, and others is growing at an even more alarming rate. While this monograph cannot be a comprehensive review, we intend that it fairly present the current state of knowledge. Our apologies for lack of space and time go to whose whose research is not reported in the pages that follow.

2
Framework for environmental analysis

CAUSES OF AND REMEDIES FOR ENVIRONMENTAL PROBLEMS

Theory of externalities
It is a fundamental principle of economic theory that the free operation of perfectly competitive markets will lead to an efficient allocation of resources in the absence of externalities. The laws of supply and demand operating in the market place will cause prices to rise or fall until at some price the quantity of each resource supplied will just equal the quantity demanded. If the price of a resource should rise, buyers will economize on its use and purchase less of it. If the price falls, the resource will be used more extravagantly. When an equilibrium price has been reached, no individual in the economy can be made better off without making some other individual worse off. Scarce resources are thus allocated efficiently and productively.

The problem is that neither environmental quality nor the pollution that degrades it is currently included in the market system. Any firm or individual may discharge wastes into the air or water without payment, subject only to existing pollution control legislation. Polluters need not pay for the harm caused by their pollution to the community around them or to downstream users of air and water. Because this resource is free, it is used more extensively than if a price were paid for its use.

This condition results in part because centuries ago, when the common law system of property allocation arose, air and water were considered to be unlimited resources. Although local pollution problems existed there was no thought that the capacity of the air and water to carry off wastes was anything but infinite. But economic growth and population growth have so increased our capacity to generate wastes that these resources are now seen to be finite and scarce, like oil, iron, and timber. Recent serious public concern about environmental quality suggests that reliance on a legal system that assumes abundance will not properly allocate a scarce resource. It cannot produce the degree of environmental quality desired by the public because that desire has no means of expression in a market.

Unsatisfactory environmental quality is a natural result of the operation of our economic system, or any other economic system without environmental legislation. The only solution to the problem is to recognize the scarcity of environmental resources and to legislate some means of allocating these resources among competing users. Governments must act to specify the rules by which waste may be discharged into the air or water. No one has suggested that we should allocate coal or steel or automobiles by a system of moral strictures and admonitions against excessive use, and it is unreasonable to suggest that such measures should be applied to such equally important resources as air and water.

Environmental quality can also be viewed as a public good – one enjoyed by all citizens (within a limited area) in equal amounts. If the environment is improved for A, it is similarly improved for his neighbour B. Neither A nor B alone will pay for a satisfactory environment because the benefits will be shared equally by those who do not pay. The private market does not adequately provide public goods, and some joint or government action is usually necessary to ensure an adequate supply.

Causes of and remedies for environmental problems have been discussed by a number of writers on the topic of external diseconomies. Viner (1931) defined a technological external diseconomy as a situation in which one party imposes costs on another party through direct physical interaction, and not through the market system. This is distinguished from a pecuniary external diseconomy in which one party imposes costs on another through market system by raising prices. For example, if smoke from A's factory reduces the output of apples from B's orchard, then B has suffered a technological external diseconomy. His output has been reduced, without any market transaction, through the direct effect of a physical relationship between the production processes of A and B. On the other hand if A's purchase of coal increases the price of coal to all consumers, because of increasing marginal costs in the coal-mining industry, then A has imposed a pecuniary external diseconomy on all other consumers. Their costs are raised, not because of direct physical interaction, but through market transactions in the purchase of coal. While Mishan (1971) finds this distinction between technological and pecuniary externalities confusing, it has been widely used. The environmental problems considered in this monograph would all be classed as technological external diseconomies.

A closely related concept is the technological external economy, in which the activity of one firm increases the output of another. An example suggested by Meade (1952) is that of an adjacent apple orchard and apiary, where the output of honey from the apiary is positively affected by increased production in the apple orchard, since more apple blossoms provide more opportunity for bees to make honey. Here the orchard owner confers a technological external economy upon the apiary operator.

Scitovsky (1954) identified four types of technological external effects: 1/ a consumer's utility may depend on the utility of other consumers; 2/a consumer's utility may depend upon the non-market activity of firms; 3/a firm's output may depend upon the non-market activity of consumers; and 4/a firm's output may depend upon the non-market activity of other firms. While interactions of the first type are important, as Scitovsky noted, they will not be discussed here since they are not considered to be environmental problems. Scitovsky said that the second interaction, which would include all pollution of consumers by producers, might be important but could easily be regulated by zoning. This dismissal was certainly premature. Many current problems and much of the literature deal with precisely this issue, which cannot always be handled by zoning since both air and water pollution can travel substantial distances. The third interaction could be represented by a farmer whose output is diminished because of air pollution from automobiles. The fourth interaction would include the fishing fleet whose output is reduced because of industrial water pollution. Scitovsky's suggestion that these categories were unimportant is disproved by the millions of dollars spent in Canada during the last decade reducing both kinds of interactions. The current outpouring of theoretical and empirical literature and the vast sums being spent both publicly and privately on interactions 2, 3, and 4 demonstrate the tremendous importance currently attached to areas which only twenty years ago could be dismissed almost completely.

A mathematical 2-firm example
A simple mathematical model proposed by Henderson and Quandt (1958) can be used to analyse pollution problems reflected by an external technological diseconomy between two producers. Suppose that two firms have cost functions C_1 and C_2 shown in the following equation:

$$C_1 = C_1(q_1, q_2), \quad C_2 = C_2(q_1, q_2), \tag{2.1}$$

where the cost for the first firm is dependent upon its own output q_1 and the output of the other firm q_2, and vice versa. The appearance of the second firm's output in the first firm's cost function might reflect the necessity for cleaning water drawn from a common pond before using it, where both firms discharge wastes into and draw water from the pond. In the absence of regulation each firm will maximize its own profits, setting price p equal to own marginal cost, as follows:

$$p = \frac{\partial C_1}{\partial q_1}, \quad p = \frac{\partial C_2}{\partial q_2}. \tag{2.2}$$

while profits for each firm depend upon activity of the other firm, neither can control the other's activity, so that each maximizes profit with respect to its own output, subject to the given output of the other firm.

In a competitive economy, in the absence of consumption externalities and assuming a satisfactory distribution of income, the social value of the product of firms 1 and 2 is the revenue accruing to the two firms. Social costs are, of course, their own costs. Social welfare is maximized by maximizing the joint profits π of the two firms:

$$\pi = \pi_1 + \pi_2 = p(q_1 + q_2) - C_1(q_1, q_2) - C_2(q_1, q_2). \tag{2.3}$$

Henderson and Quandt find that the first-order conditions for maximizing social welfare in equation (2.3) are satisfied as follows:

$$p = \frac{\partial C_1}{\partial q_1} + \frac{\partial C_2}{\partial q_1}, \quad p = \frac{\partial C_1}{\partial q_2} + \frac{\partial C_2}{\partial q_2}. \tag{2.4}$$

This equation states that the price for firm 1 should equal the marginal cost to firm 1 of its own production plus the cost imposed on firm 2 by an additional unit of output from firm 1. Similarly, the price for firm 2 should equal its private marginal cost for producing another unit of output plus the cost imposed on firm 1 by another unit of output from firm 2. Thus maximizing social welfare no longer requires that price equal private marginal cost. In the presence of external diseconomies, price must equal marginal *social* costs if a welfare maximum is to be reached. The difference between equations (2.2) and (2.4) is the difference between private marginal costs and social marginal costs. If firm 1 is operating on the increasing portion of its marginal cost curve, then the addition of the second term to its price equation means that it must produce at a lower private marginal cost than before, and therefore produce a smaller output. Thus the socially desirable output from a polluting firm is less than the output level that would be arrived at by the competitive market mechanism in the absence of regulation.

If this were an external economy rather than diseconomy (as in the case of Meade's apples and honey) then $\partial C_2/\partial q_1$ would be negative rather than positive.

At a given output price this would require a higher private marginal cost of production than in the private profit maximizing situation, and therefore a greater output. Thus the source of a technological external economy must produce at a greater level of output for social welfare maximization than for private profit maximization. Similar results for both cases would be achieved if we replaced firm 2 with a consumer.

This example demonstrates that social welfare will be improved if a polluter is compelled to reduce his polluting activity below the amount that would occur in a perfectly competitive private market. He should produce at the point where his sales price equals the marginal social cost of an additional unit of output. One way to achieve this result would be to force him to pay for the damage caused by his pollution. If this external effect is recognized in a market transaction, then private profit maximization will require establishing output such that the price equals the marginal cost of production plus the marginal damage that must be compensated. In other words, levying a tax schedule upon the producer equal to his marginal damage will automatically bring his production into a welfare maximizing position. If the polluter is faced with a price for his pollution output, he is then free to choose between reducing output and installing pollution controls in order to maximize his own profits. With such a tax, private profit maximizing behaviour is once again consistent with social welfare maximization. It is clear, however, that the government or some other body must act to impose a tax if this welfare maximum is to be achieved.

Negotiated solutions

While we have talked thus far about a two-firm situation, we have assumed that there is no interaction between the firms except through their polluting activities. That is, direct negotiation between them was ruled out. In the case of two firms, however, it seems most likely that when they discovered the extent to which their costs were affected by each other's production they would negotiate to improve their joint profit position. To simplify the example, suppose that only firm 1 causes pollution, which reduces output from firm 2. Figure 1 shows the marginal gain to firm 1 from emitting pollution as line *DB*. In the absence of regulation or negotiation, the firm will operate at point *B* where the marginal gain from further pollution is zero. Line *AE* shows the marginal damage to firm 2 from that pollution. In the absence of regulation or negotiation, firm 2 will suffer marginal damage of *BE,* and total damage equal to the area under line *AE,* or *AEB*.

Suppose that representatives of the two firms meet to negotiate some improvement in their over-all position. Since firm 2 can save amount *BE* for the first unit of pollution controlled by firm 1, and the cost of that control is nearly zero, firm 2 would be prepared to offer any amount up to *BE* as a bribe for

Figure 1
Gains and damages from pollution by Firm 1

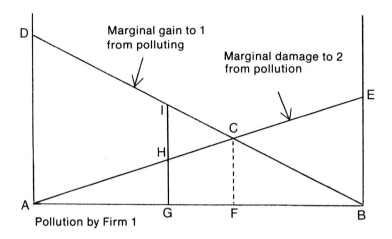

reduced emissions. Firm 1 would accept any amount over zero for that reduction. Thus, beginning at point *B*, the firms would negotiate to the left toward lower and lower emissions. To the left of point *C* the damage to firm 2 from a unit of pollution is below the marginal gain to firm 1 from that pollution. Here firm 2 is no longer prepared to offer more to firm 1 than the private cost of controlling pollution. Thus movement will stop at point *C*, with emissions of *AF* remaining and *FB* controlled.

The savings to firm 2 from this reduction are the area *FCEB*. The cost to firm 1 will be triangle *FCB*. The amount of the bribe will be indeterminant, but must be greater than *FCB* and less than *FCEB*. The triangle *CEB* represents the net improvement in profits for the two firms, which is the net reduction in social costs associated with the pollution. Since there is a mutual advantage to moving from point *B* to point *F*, these negotiations will take place assuming that the transactions costs are small relative to the gains *CEB*.

The same result would occur if the firms had started at point *A* rather than at point *B*. Suppose that because of law or tradition firm 1 was required to control all of its emissions, and therefore started at point *A*. Firm 1 would recognize that its savings from emitting the first units of pollution are far greater than the marginal damage caused to firm 2. It would thus suggest movement to the right from point *A* and offer to firm 2 bribes that were above line *AE* but below *DB*. If the firms again move to point *F*, firm 2 will suffer damage of *ACF* but firm 1 will save *ADCF*. Here a bribe will be paid by firm 1 to firm 2 for allowing it to pollute *AF,* and the bribe will be somewhere between *ACF* and *ADCF.* The triangle *ADC* represents the social gain from allowing this pollution, which will be split between the two firms according to their bargaining power. Once again, social welfare has been improved.

Thus, in the case of two parties causing and suffering a technological external diseconomy, private profit maximizing motives will lead to negotiation from either zero control or complete control to the amount of pollution that minimizes social costs. Where negotiation can take place, no government intervention is necessary. The firms will by themselves reach the optimal position as indicated by Turvey (1963). Only where information and negotiation costs (transaction costs) are substantial relative to the externality, will an externality lead to market failure in the two-party case.

The bilateral nature of externality
Coase (1960) proposed that a reduction in emissions could be reached by negotiating either from point *A* or point *B* and suggested pollution control laws as a starting point for negotiation. If the law prohibits all emissions, two parties to a pollution problem may begin negotiating at point *A* in Figure 1 to find their joint profit maximizing pollution level. If only the two parties are affected by the emission, there is no reason for anyone else to enforce the law requiring zero emissions. If, on the other hand, the law imposes no limits on emissions, the parties begin with the rights defined at point *B.* The pollutee must bribe the polluter to reduce his emissions, rather than receiving compensation for suffering emissions. In either case, negotiation will lead to emissions at point *F.* The difference is in who pays whom to arrive at that point. Coase argues that while there are distributional differences between the two legal positions, resource allocation should be essentially unchanged as long as the pollutee has an incentive to minimize his damage when he has the right to compensation. He implicitly assumes a constant marginal utility of money (no income effect on consumers) and ignores the effect of different profit levels on production decisions in the long run, both of which could shift both curves depending on the assignment of the environmental right.

A polluter is typically thought of as a wrongdoer who has injured someone else by causing emissions. Coase suggests that either party might equally be regarded as a wrongdoer. While in the absence of the polluter the pollutees would suffer no damage, in the absence of pollutees there would no reason for the polluter to limit his emissions. When regulations are imposed the recipients of the pollution have damaged the polluter by insisting that he clean up his wastes. Thus either party can impose costs on the other. To say that one is a wrongdoer assumes that there is some moral justification for assigning environmental rights either to the polluter or to the pollutee. This is most apparent in the negotiated situation where, Coase argues, the same environmental result is reached whether the law prohibits pollution or allows it without restriction. The primary consequence of pollution control laws in the Coase situation is to shift the original rights from one party to the other, and therefore to change the direction and magnitude of the bribe. While we may wish to make moral judgments about who should be allowed to make what use of the environment, it should be recognized that in doing so we are assigning property rights.

While the bilaterial nature of the costs is important to recognize, the argument that the legal assignment of rights is irrelevent to resource allocation goes too far. It ignores income effects by implicitly assuming a constant marginal utility of money, otherwise the income consequences of property right assignments would affect consumption patterns and thereby resource allocation. Much more serious, it neglects the impact of liability rules on profits of the firms. If the polluter is bribed to reduce his emissions he may pollute no more than if he paid an effluent charge, but his profits will be higher. Either he must lower his product price, thereby increasing his sales volume, or other firms will be attracted by the profits, enter the industry, and gather similar bribes while increasing total production. Even if environmental quality is independent of liability, the output of the firm to which the environmental right is initially assigned will be greater then if it bore the liability instead, unless very restrictive assumptions are made about the parties. Finally, the argument ignores a pollutee's ability to reduce his damages by protective action that he would have no incentive to pursue if he were fully compensated.

The problem in applying Coase's arguments to actual cases is that the requisite conditions for negotiation rarely occur. Negotiation is only a reasonable solution where very few parties are involved, so that the transaction costs of determining pollution quantities, consequences, and compensation are small and problems of public goods and revealed preference do not arise. Most current environmental problems, however, involve large numbers of polluters or pollutees or both, often thousands of both in urban areas. Here the idea of negotiation between the affected parties is absurd. Only in the occasional case of a single factory and a large farmer or a single factory and a fisherman's association is there much likelihood of reaching the efficient negotiated solution envisaged by Coase. And negotiation can be quite expensive even between only two parties. In most real situations, negotiation has not occurred and cannot take place. The rights usually exercised are those provided originally by law, and there is no deviation from them. Thus one must consider carefully to whom the law should initially assign environmental rights.

Policy choice in non-negotiable cases

The mathematical model above indicated that social welfare is maximized when the quantity of output and pollution from a polluter is such that the price of his product is just equal to his private marginal cost for production plus any external social costs of production. In a competitive economy this optimal point can be reached by imposing on the polluter an effluent charge equal to the marginal social cost of his pollution. If there are many pollutees rather than one, negotiation costs render negotiation unlikely, and the revealed preference problem arising out of the public good nature of environmental quality destroys any hope of negotiation. Government action is necessary. Figure 1 shows that an effluent charge levied according to a schedule that produced line *AE* would result in the optimal degree of pollution *AF*. Similarly, if regulation prohibited emissions beyond point *F* the environmental result would be identical. However, prices affect income and therefore both product demand and entry into an industry. It is unlikely that a set of standards would achieve the same pollution level as an effluent charge *and* yield the same product output. If standards and charges achieve the same environmental result, the effluent charge should yield a lower product output from the polluting industry.

What should be done with revenues collected from an effluent charge? In general, it is collection of the charge that causes the optimal allocation of resources. Whether the charge is paid into general revenues or used for other public purposes is irrelevant. In one circumstance, however, the revenue from the effluent charge should be paid to the pollutee. Suppose that there is only one polluter and one pollutee, but that the government nevertheless intervenes to impose an effluent charge. This charge, if correctly computed, would lead firm 1 to emit amount *AF* in Figure 1. Since the parties can negotiate, however, firm 2, which is still suffering marginal damages of *FC*, will be inclined to offer firm 1 a bribe to further reduce its emissions. The marginal net cost to firm 1 of further reductions is the difference between its marginal gain curve *DB* and the schedule of effluent charges it must pay *AE*. Thus at point *F* it will accept an infinitesimal amount in exchange for a small reduction in emissions. Since firm 2 would be prepared to pay *CF*, the firms will move to the left of point *F*. This movement will continue until the net marginal gain to firm 1, the difference between *DB* and *AE*, is just equal to the marginal damage to firm 2, line *AE*. This would be at a point like *G*, where *GH* equals *HI*. Thus imposition of an effluent charge in a situation where the parties can negotiate will lead to excessive pollution reduction. The only way to avoid this result is to pay the revenues from the effluent charge to firm 2. Then when firm 1 reduces emission, firm 2 loses revenue in just the amount of the effluent charge. By this mechanism the government acts as an intermediary performing negotiations the firms could undertake themselves. It is a superfluous effort, but at least it leads to the optimal solution *AF*. In the absence of negotiation, as Kneese and Bower (1968, 99-100) indicate, there would be no reason to pay the revenues to the pollutee.

ENVIRONMENTAL POLICY OBJECTIVES

The works discussed in the previous section all indicated that in the absence of government regulation, and where no negotiation between polluter and pollutee is possible, environmental problems will arise. These problems will consist of pollution levels greater than would be socially desirable. Many of the writers define the desirable or optimal pollution levels in terms of costs, benefits, or prices, and some suggest policies that would lead to achieving these optimal levels. Here we will consider several objectives for environmental policies, criteria against which alternative policies can be evaluated.

The studies considered above define a 'solution' to the environmental problem in terms of a single criterion: maximizing social welfare. We will refer to this criterion as 'social efficiency,' which means achieving a pollution control level such that any further control would impose abatement costs greater than the savings in pollution damage or welfare benefits that would result. If it is not possible to define a social welfare function, then the objective can be stated in terms of Pareto optimality, or Pareto efficiency. Pareto efficiency requires pollution control until the point at which no person could be made better off by more or less pollution without making others worse off.

Another criterion that appears frequently is that of minimizing the cost of achieving a given degree of pollution control. A number of studies, notably Johnson (1967), assume some environmental quality standard and attempt to determine the least costly means of achieving that standard. We shall refer to this objective as a search for 'abatement efficiency,' which takes the environmental quality standard or goal as given and examines only the cost of meeting that goal. Since the empirical determination of optimal pollution control levels is extremely difficult, the search for abatement efficiency must, as a practical matter, frequently replace a search for social efficiency.

None of the above studies and little of the literature on pollution control discuss measurement costs or administrative expenses. A brief review of the budget allocation of pollution control authorities and discussions with enforcement officers, however, suggest that the cost of monitoring and surveillance is enormously important in determining actual environmental policies. Thus a third objective of any realistic policy should be administrative efficiency. We should seek to achieve a given level of control at the least possible administrative cost, or strike a balance between the costs of abatement, the benefits of reduced emissions, and the costs of administering a program. A later chapter will deal exclusively with measurement problems.

A fourth objective is the promotion of technological progress. While some types of pollution control have been used for decades and change very slowly, in many cases one could expect great improvements in control technology if proper incentives were applied. For example, Dewees (1974) demonstrates that auto- mobile pollution control costs have dropped rapidly since the first introduction of controls in 1968. If technological progress can reduce total control costs by a factor of two or more, it is important to select policies that will foster more rapid progress. In the long run this may be much more important than selecting the 'correct' degree of abatement or the efficient allocation of that burden among polluters.

A final objective of any emission control program deals with the distribution of control costs among polluters and of benefits among pollutees. In any area where there are many sources of pollution one could devise many different allocations of the responsibility for abatement to meet a given environmental standard. The criterion of abatement efficiency would suggest allocating the burden to minimize total costs. This, however, might cause firms that are otherwise quite similar to suffer vastly different abatement costs or percentages of abatement. As a practical political matter it is important to consider whether the distribution of costs is fair or equitable to the various polluters. And since the geographic distribution of pollution is not uniform it is also important to consider the equity of various policies as they affect the pollutees. While economic theory provides little guidance on the relative fairness or equity of different distributions of costs and benefits, at a minimum it is important to describe for each policy how these occur. As in the case of income distribution, the theory may not suggest a choice among programs on equity grounds, but the distributional consequences can be described, so that the political process, where such considerations are vitally important, has adequate information on which to operate.

One problem implicit in many environmental policy considerations, but not explicitly discussed in the five criteria above, is that of uncertainty. Information about the costs of pollution control or the consquences of continued emissions is often poor. Policy must be made without a definite understanding of the comparative consequences for human health or economic growth of alternative policies. Although much of the theoretical literature treats environmental prob- lems as if perfect information were available, this is not a useful description of most real world problems. Thus consideration of objectives must include some treat- ment of risk and uncertainty. The concept of decision-making under uncertainty and the tools of state-preference analysis may be useful in evaluating different policies according to these criteria. Maximizing social welfare, or social efficiency, may in some cases reduce to determining which policies will minimize the risk of serious environmental harm at a reasonable cost. It may be as important to design policies that will avoid a small possibility of a catastrophic disaster as to balance costs and benefits of the most likely outcomes.

Most of the present discussion will refer to the first two objectives, social efficiency and abatement efficiency, because most studies have discussed how much pollution should be allowed or how the burden of meeting certain standards should be allocated among polluters. Where sufficient information is available, however, we shall discuss the other three criteria, since they appear to be important for policy-making. Particular attention is paid to all five criteria in chapter 6, where alternative policies are specifically compared.

HOW MUCH POLLUTION IS DESIRABLE?

Balancing costs and benefits
Of the five suggested criteria for evaluating environmental policies, only the first deals with determining the proper amount of total emissions. We can see from the simple model proposed by Henderson and Quandt (1958) that joint profits of two firms are maximized when each adjusts its output and pollution levels until the price of its product is just equal to its private marginal cost of production plus the social marginal cost of its pollution. To generalize this: social welfare is maximized when pollution is controlled until the point at which the marginal cost to the polluter of further control is just equal to the marginal cost of further emissions. In short, the optimal pollution level is that at which the marginal benefit of further emission control just equals the marginal cost of that control. This is point F in Figure 1.

Most of the literature discussed so far involves continuous production functions and damage or benefit functions such as those shown in Figure 1. In such cases we can talk about continuous variation in the emission level until the precise point is reached where the two margins are equated. For many polluters and many pollutees the relevant curves are a marginal cost curve that is the horizontal sum of individual control cost curves and a marginal benefit curve that is the vertical sum of benefits to all who are affected. Once these curves are derived the optimal point can easily be determined. This means that to define a satisfactory solution we must be able to determine empirically marginal control cost functions and marginal damage or benefit functions.

In some cases, however, smooth functions are not available. For example, should a new power station burn high-sulphur coal or much cleaner natural gas? This is essentially a discrete choice, not a continuous one. Alternatively, the decision may be whether or not to build a sewage treatment plant for a given city, or whether to design it for primary, secondary, or tertiary treatment. Again, the choices will be discrete rather than continuous.

Here the relevent decision process involves cost-benefit analysis. We can treat the choice of boiler fuels or construction of the sewage treatment plant as a project for which cost-benefit calculations can be made. Taking the present value of costs for the project over a reasonable lifetime and comparing them with the present value of benefits from that project one can determine whether or not it should be undertaken. There is a clear analogy between this cost-benefit analysis of large projects and the comparison of continuous marginal benefit and marginal cost curves for continuously variable functions. In either case further pollution control should be undertaken until the costs of additional control outweigh the benefits. Chapters 3 and 4 discuss in detail the methodology available for determining costs and benefits in different environmental situations and present some empirical results for common environmental problems.

Costs can often be estimated with some accuracy, but benefits elude quantification. In such cases an environmental quality goal may be set, albeit somewhat arbitrarily. The analytical problem in these cases is to meet the quality goal with the least cost — to achieve abatement efficiency. Here cost-benefit analysis is replaced by cost-effectiveness analysis, which compares the cost per unit of abatement for a variety of technologies or policies.

Sometimes, however, the appropriate policy is not limited emissions but absolute prohibition. For several years DDT has been banned for many agricultural uses, and the discharge of mercury and other heavy metals into water is frequently completely prohibited. Upon further examination these cases may nevertheless be consistent with the principle of balancing costs and benefits. Mercury, chromium, and other heavy metals are highly toxic, able to destroy some forms of life at very low concentrations. They do not degrade over time and can be concentrated through the food chain so that even low rates of emission may lead to high concentration in certain animals after a sufficient period of time. Because of their persistence the damages from their emissions are potentially quite high. The special case of pollutants that accumulate over time is discussed later in this chapter.

On the cost side, such toxic materials are frequently emitted by only a small fraction of all water-using activities. And it is often true that some alternative process is available in which the material is not even present, or that a highly efficient recovery mechanism can be designed. If the costs of control are not unreasonable and the potential damages are enormous, an outright prohibition may properly reflect the balancing of large benefits against moderate costs. In the case of highly toxic materials, or persistent materials which may be concentrated over time, complete prohibition of discharge may be entirely consistent with the objective of social efficiency. It is important to remember, however, that efficiency is the ultimate objective, against which any proposed prohibition should be tested. Reducing emissions below the level at which they are harmful or perceptible or both would be hard to justify on any economic grounds.

The role of dispersion

One problem in comparing benefits and costs of a particular pollution control strategy is establishing the basis upon which the comparison is to be made. Most pollution control cost functions are for an individual plant, specifying the dollars or cents per ton, gram, or other measure of pollutant required to prevent its release to the air or water. Benefits of abatement or pollution damage, however, result, not from a unit of pollution emitted, but from a unit of pollution in the environment. Most benefit studies will therefore specify, if they provide any empirical results, a change in benefits related to a change in ambient pollution concentrations. Comparing costs and benefits requires conversion of emission rates into ambient quality. Such conversion is usually done with a dispersion model that is particularly adapted to the physical situation in question.

First, suppose that two firms located on a smoothly flowing river discharge into that river a pollutant that does not degrade or change in concentration over time. Firm 1 discharges this pollutant at rate d_1 and firm 2 discharges at rate d_2, as shown in Figure 2. If the stream is narrow and well mixed we can assume that pollution concentrations are uniform through any cross-section of the stream. Ambient pollution concentrations in this stream would be a direct function of the rate of discharge into the stream. The functional relationship could be either derived from engineering theory or measured empirically. For example, in Figure 2, the ambient concentration c_1 at the bathing beach would be a function of the rate of discharge by firm 1, as follows:

$$c_1(t) = f[d_1(t)]. \tag{2.5}$$

If the emission rate d_1 varied, so would the concentration at c_1, but with a time-lag related to the flow of the stream. The pollutant concentration at time t at the fishing spot c_3 would be a function of the discharge rates by firms 1 and 2 as follows:

$$c_3(t) = f[d_1(t), d_2(t)]. \tag{2.6}$$

If pollutants from the two firms do not interact, concentration c_3 should reflect a summation of the contributions of the two firms:

$$c_3(t) = f_1[d_1(t)] + f_2[d_2(t)]. \tag{2.7}$$

Figure 2
Dispersion of pollution in a stream

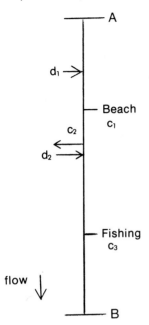

Finally, if discharge rates are constant over time, the concentration c_3 will be constant and proportional to the two discharges. Equation (2.8) shows the steady-state concentrations at points 1 and 3 as a function of discharges from sources 1 and 2, where $a_1{}^3$ is the relation between emissions from source 1 and ambient concentration at point 3.

$$c_1 = a_1{}^1 d_1, \quad c_3 = a_1{}^3 d_1 + a_2{}^3 d_2. \tag{2.8}$$

The benefits of reducing d_2 by a single unit would equal the benefit of reducing ambient concentration c_3 times coefficient $a_2{}^3$. The diffusion or transport coefficient a can be used to translate ambient concentration into discharge concentration or vice versa. It is essential for any comparison of pollution control costs and benefits from ambient quality improvement.

If the pollutant is a conservative one, so that its concentration in the stream does not change as it flows, water quality will be uniform from discharge d_1 to discharge d_2, and uniform again from discharge d_2 down to the end of the stream, point B. On the other hand, if the pollutant degrades over time, which is more common, concentration will be a function not only of the discharge rate but also of distance from the discharge. Thus, even with steady-state discharge at rates d_1 and d_2, water quality will vary throughout the stream, although in a predictable manner. Once again, coefficients of the type shown in equation (2.8) can be derived, but these would have to be determined separately for every point along the stream. Their use to relate source and ambient concentrations is the same as with a conservative pollutant. They still represent a means of translating a unit of discharge into a change in ambient quality. Dorfman and Jacoby (1972) describe an example analysing a stream with several discharges and several water users according to a number of objective functions. Clearly one cannot decide how much total abatement is required in a stream unless one knows the transfer or dispersion coefficient that relates discharge to ambient quality.

Determining the relationship between emission rates and ambient concentrations becomes more difficult when dealing with an atmospheric problem or a large lake instead of a flowing stream. Complex atmospheric models have been used to determine air quality as a function of emission from a particular point, and a variety of models used to simulate the currents and dispersion in lakes. Suppose, for example, that Figure 3 represents a lake with pollution discharged at rates d_3 and d_4, affecting recreational areas with concentration c_3 and c_4. A complex model would be needed to predict concentrations c_3 and c_4 as a function of the two discharge rates. With conservative pollutants the relationships would depend upon currents and dispersion rates. With non-conservative pollutants many other factors would be involved, including water temperature and biological activity. If many sources and receptors are located on the lake a large number of equations would be necessary to make the relevant predictions.

If the lake is small and well mixed some simplifying assumptions can be applied. If the total discharge of a certain pollutant into the lake, and the average quality of the lake are known, a fixed percentage reduction in total discharge might be assumed to result in the same percentage reduction in ambient concentration. While this makes strong assumptions about the linearity of the transfer functions, it vastly simplifies the computational problem.

The same simplifying assumption of a perfectly mixed body has been used in the case of air pollution. For example, the United States auto emission standards assume that a percentage reduction in total automotive emissions for a city can be translated into a corresponding percentage reduction in ambient pollution concentrations for the atmosphere over that city (Ingram 1975a). The translation of a change in total emission into a change in ambient air quality by this simple technique is referred to as a 'rollback' model. It assumes that if emissions are rolled back 10 per cent concentrations are also reduced by 10 per cent. This

Figure 3
Dispersion in a lake or airshed

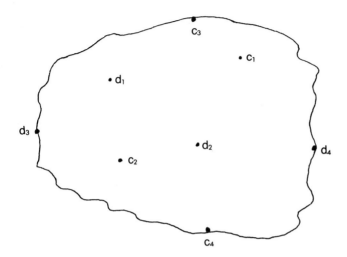

model is best applied when the flow of pollution is large relative to the stock in the atmosphere or water body, and when many sources are uniformly spread over a large area in which benefits are to be accrued. These conditions are met for automobiles in cities, but they are less applicable to most water pollution situations.

Much more sophisticated models have also been applied to air pollution problems. Ingram (1975b) describes an urban air quality model in which stationary and mobile sources are represented in the appropriate geographic locations. Meteorological conditions are simulated to determine ambient air quality at all points in the city resulting from any dispersed set of emissions. The model can therefore determine the change in air quality at any one of hundreds of points in the city resulting from a change in emission rate from a single smoke stack, from automobiles in the central business district, or from automobiles throughout the metropolitan area. This allows determination of the benefits of emission rates and air quality.

Suppose that we have an estimate of the total damage in Lake Ontario from water pollution for an average year. The benefits from uniformly reducing all emissions into the lake by a given percentage may be estimated by using a simple rollback model in which 10 per cent less emissions means 10 per cent less pollution to determine how much damage would be reduced by this improvement in ambient quality. If we want to evaluate a reduction in discharge from a specific source, however, we must either know what damages are currently caused by that source, or how this reduction would affect ambient quality in all areas of the lake. Even with a dispersion model that would translate reduced emissions into improved water quality we would need to know how the damages were distributed through the lake, so that a portion of the total damage figure could be attributed to the predicted improvements in local water quality. Thus, even in cases where total damage from pollutants can be estimated and the abatement cost for a particular source is known, we may be far from comparing marginal costs and marginal benefits for that source. A thorough analysis may involve detailed use of very expensive dispersion models before the appropriate comparisons can be made. In chapters 3 and 4, where benefits and costs of control are discussed, specific reference is made to the problem of producing both figures on a basis that allows them to be compared for policy evaluation.

STOCKS AND FLOWS OF POLLUTION

The previous analysis has dealt with conservative and degrading pollutants and with mixed and unmixed receiving waters or air masses. We have always assumed, however, that the concentration of pollution in the environment was a direct function only of the current flow of emissions. This allowed determination of the ambient pollution concentration q at any point as a function only of the emission rates e of the relevant sources.

This relationship may be perfectly appropriate for local air pollution in a city or for water pollution in a river. In either case, even if the pollutant is conservative, the concentration at one point will be steady, given a uniform flow and uniform rate of discharge. The rollback dispersion model, so often used in economic analyses, is perfectly appropriate in these situations.

But there are important environmental problems where this relationship is not appropriate. Carbon dioxide concentrations in the atmosphere have increased enormously since the turn of the century. While there are processes to remove carbon dioxide from the atmosphere, they apparently operate much less rapidly than the rate of discharge. Thus the concentration of carbon dioxide at any time is related not to the emission rate at that time but to the sum of emissions over many previous years. The damage is done by the stock of pollution in the atmosphere which is only in the long run related to the flow of pollution discharge.

When discharged into a water course mercury is only slowly removed, and then primarily as sediment on the bottom of the river or lake. Here it can enter marine organisms and begin to move up the food chain to plants and fish. The concentration of mercury in water, in sediment, or in marine life will be a function of this year's emissions and the emissions of many previous years. Many other conservative substances such as DDT either have no removal mechanism, do not degrade over time, or are removed or degraded over a period of many years. In any of these cases, in a closed system, the ambient concentration will depend not on current emissions but on the recent history of emissions.

In a flowing stream the concentration of pollutants q is a function of a set of I individual emission rates e:

$$q = f(e_i), \quad i = 1 \dots I. \tag{2.9}$$

With a conservative or accumulating pollutant in a fixed reservoir, the ambient concentration or stock of pollution at a specific point in time t_1 will be a function of historic emission rates:

$$q_{t_1} = f(e_{it}), \quad i = 1 \dots I, \; t = 0 \dots t_2. \tag{2.10}$$

Thus current ambient quality is a function of previous emissions; current emissions affect future as well as current ambient quality.

In the case where emissions and ambient quality were independent from one year to the next, welfare was maximized by minimizing the sum of pollution control costs and pollution damage in that year. The condition for this cost-minimization was that marginal benefits of control equal marginal costs of control. When different years can no longer be regarded as independent, some time-dependent decision-making process must be adopted. If a series of decisions must be made to arrive at an optimal pollution discharge rate for every year, then the set of decisions could be regarded as components of a pollution control project. The project can be evaluated in traditional cost-benefit terms: minimize the present value of the sum of pollution control costs and pollution damages, with future years discounted to the present at a discount rate. This is shown in equation 2.11 where t_1 is the beginning of the period of analysis, T represents the time horizon of the analysis, $C_{it}(e_{it})$ is the cost of pollution control in year t for source i, and $D_t(q_t)$ is the damage done in year t by ambient pollution concentration q; The discount rate is r:

$$\text{Min} \sum_{t=t_1}^{T} \left[\sum_{i=1}^{T} C_{it}(e_{it}) + D_t(q_t) \right] \frac{1}{(1+r)^{t-t_1}}. \tag{2.11}$$

The optimal time path for pollution control, emissions, and ambient quality depend here upon the shapes of all relevant curves and also upon the relationship between pollution control costs in different years. If pollution control is achieved by major discrete investments, control costs in one year will be strongly dependent upon investments and costs in previous years. In such cases, solution of the minimization problem shown in equation 3 is a difficult programming problem that cannot be described in general terms. Keeler, Spence, and Zeckhauser (1971) have solved a similar problem, but under a very limiting set of assumptions.

It would be useful however, to explore the optimal time path of emissions and environmental quality for an accumulating pollutant. This is possible if some simplifying assumptions are applied. Consider a single lake into which a perfectly conservative pollutant is discharged. The lake is perfectly mixed, and there is no removal mechanism, so that the concentration of pollution is uniform across the lake and at any time depends only upon current and past emissions from a single source. In this case the pollution density at any time can be expressed as:

$$q_{t_1} = a \int_0^{t_1} e(t) \, dt,$$ (2.12)

where a is a dispersion coefficient for the pollutant.

Assume further that the damages caused in a single year are a function only of the pollution level in that year. Damage caused in previous years has no influence on this year's damage. We can express the pollution damage d_t as in equation 2.13:

$$d_{t_1} = d(q_{t_1}).$$ (2.13)

Assume that damages increase more rapidly than concentration, which implies a positive first derivative for equation 2.13 and increasing marginal damages with concentration. This assumption of independent damages in each year is not appropriate for many kinds of pollution except at rather low levels. If pollution is sufficient in one year to eliminate some species of plants or animals from the area, they are not likely to reform in full strength the next year, and the damage function will therefore be somewhat different. This assumption may be acceptable, however, in cases of moderate pollution damage which occurs during one season of a year. Thus air pollution might affect the crop of apples in an orchard one year, but not be sufficient to damage the trees themselves. In a succeeding year, the potential crop of apples would be unchanged, and the damage would depend only on the pollution density in this second year.

Finally, assume that the cost of pollution control in year t_1 is a simple function of the emissions in that year alone, and increase more rapidly than the degree of abatement so that marginal abatement costs increase with decreasing emissions. This is shown in equation 2.14:

$$c_{t_1} = c(e_{t_1}).$$
(2.14)

The independent cost functions in each year suggest that pollution control is achieved without major fixed investments. One could think of the control being achieved by capital equipment with a life of only one year, or with inputs of only labour and material.

We can now consider an optimal policy of pollution control for the simple system described by equations 2.12 through 2.14. 'Optimal' is defined as minimizing the present value of pollution control costs plus pollution damage costs over the life of the analysis.

Some indication of optimal pollution control in this system can be derived from considering a first year and a subsequent year in isolation. In the first year of analysis, if pollution has just begun, the ambient pollution level $q(1)$ will be very small. This implies low marginal damages for that year, that is, low marginal benefits of abatement. In the tenth year, because of emissions in years one through nine, $q(10)$ will be substantially greater than $q(1)$. If the time horizon for analysis is long enough, the present value of marginal benefits calculated from year 1 and discounted at a reasonable rate will be lower than the present value of marginal benefits beginning in year ten because the pollution level in the second case will always be higher than in the first case. If the present value of marginal benefits after year ten is greater than the present value of marginal benefits after year one then a greater degree of pollution control is required for year ten than for year one. In short, marginal abatement costs in a given year can be equated to the present value of marginal benefits from that abatement for all future years. Since pollution levels must necessarily rise, marginal benefits necessarily rise over time, and therefore the appropriate degree of abatement will increase.

The emission rate thus begins at some positive value e_1 and declines over time. So long as e is positive q will increase over time. If at zero emissions the marginal cost is significant and if marginal damages rise to a sufficiently high level, then at some time the marginal damages from another unit of abatement will be greater than the marginal costs of 100 per cent abatement. If this happens optimal emissions will be zero at that time, and ambient quality should be held constant thereafter.

If this corner solution is not reached, then the emission rate e_t will decline asymptotically to zero, while the ambient pollution concentration $q(t)$ will increase asymptotically to either some fixed value or some fixed rate of increase, depending upon how rapidly e approaches zero.

In summary, if a conservative pollutant is discharged into a fixed reservoir, and if the marginal damage and marginal cost functions are identical in all years, then the optimal pollution control policy is to allow some finite emissions initially, and reduce that emission rate over time. The environment will become more polluted until some equilibrium is reached at which emissions are zero or negligibly small and ambient concentrations are essentially constant. If pollution control costs are not independent among years, there will be non-linearities and discrete increments in pollution abatement but the general nature of the solution should not be affected. If marginal damages are not independent in each year, it is difficult to say what policy would be optimal.

There are several reasons why actual policies might differ from the theoretical set just described. First, if the population grows over time, the marginal damage curve may shift upward as more people utilize the resource being polluted. The abatement cost curve could shift up because of increased demand for the polluters' products. On the other hand, technical progress in emission control might shift that cost curve down over time. Finally tastes may change over time. If incomes rise so that people have more leisure time in which to contemplate and enjoy the environment, demand for environmental quality may rise. Thus a level of pollution that is optimal for one generation may be entirely unacceptable for another.

There is a tendency for resources of the kind described here to be diminished over time. If a pollutant is indeed persistent, the total quantity in the environment must inevitably accumulate over time as emissions appear in new places and continue for several years until controls can be instituted. Thus substitutes for a clear lake may become less available. This would tend to shift upward the demand curve for this lake, and therefore increase the damages from any emission level.

The role of the discount rate in this time path of emissions must be seriously considered. The higher the discount rate, the less heavily future damages weigh in current considerations, and therefore the greater the initial rate of pollution emissions. In addition, a higher discount rate might postpone the time at which zero emissions are reached. Thus a high discount rate always means a dirtier environment.

A very low discount rate will tend to reduce emissions at all times throughout the analysis. In fact, if a zero discount rate is applied, with positive marginal benefits at low ambient concentrations and finite marginal costs at low emission rates the optimal policy would be zero emissions throughout the entire period. With a zero discount rate, any finite benefits multiplied by an infinite time horizon yields infinite benefits. Thus the preservationists' argument for zero emissions can be sustained by arguing for a zero discount rate in cases where the pollutant is clearly accumulating.

This analysis suggests that there are some respects in which Meadows and Meadows (1972) were properly alarmed about pollution problems. First, even a degrading pollutant that does not accumulate over time must be controlled to a greater and greater degree as the affected population increases and as the economic activity generating the pollutant increases. In the absence of techno- logical progress, total pollution control costs associated with the optimal policy will rise over time. In the case of an accumulating pollutant, things are even worse. Even a static economy with no growth will experience rising optimal pollution control costs. A growing economy could face a quite rapidly increasing pollution control requirement.

The challenge presented by these facts is clear. It is imperative that techno- logical progress in pollution control occur if we are to avoid at some time the choice between ecological disaster and enormous pollution control expenditures. The requisite technological progress may occur, but only if there are sufficient incentives for the research and development to produce more efficient tech- nology at lower costs. Thus it is essential to design pollution control programs providing such incentives.

ALLOCATION OF ABATEMENT RESPONSIBILITY

In an area with numerous source of pollution the determination of desirable air quality, based upon costs and benefits of abatement, does not solve the policy- makers' problem. It is still necessary to determine how much of the abatement should be undertaken by each of the several sources of pollution. Imagine a perfectly mixed pond or airshed, so that one pound of pollutant has an equal impact on ambient quality throughout the area regardless of who discharged it. Suppose, further, that several firms of similar size discharge similar amounts of pollution but have different abatement costs. Firm 1 can clean up 90 per cent of its pollution at a marginal cost of ten cents per pound and an average cost of three cents per pound, while firm 2 can clean up only 10 per cent of its pollu- tion at a 10-cent marginal cost: 90 per cent control for firm 2 would cost fifteen cents per pound on average. In such a case abatement efficiency (minimizing the cost of achieving a given improvement in ambient quality) will best be served by imposing most of the clean-up responsibility on firm 1 and only a small amount on firm 2. As Kneese and Bower (1968, 63) have shown, a given total emission reduction will be achieved at least cost if each source abates until all experience equal marginal abatement costs. Just as the lowest-cost means of producing a good occurs when all firms experience equal marginal costs, so the lowest-cost means of preventing pollution is achieved when all producers experience equal marginal pollution control costs. In Figure 4 the curves represent the marginal pollution control costs for firms 1 and 2. The area under the curves from the left

Figure 4
Marginal costs of pollution control for two firms

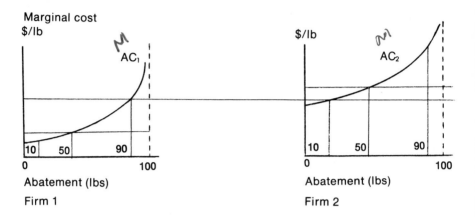

Marginal cost
$/lb

AC₁

Abatement (lbs)

Firm 1

$/lb

AC₂

Abatement (lbs)

Firm 2

is the total cost of pollution control. If one hundred pounds must be abated it is less expensive to abate ninety pounds from firm 1 and ten pounds from firm 2 than, for example, to abate fifty pounds from each.

While equating marginal costs may satisfy abatement efficiency, it could easily offend one's sense of equity. Firm 1 in Figure 4 has lower costs for any degree of abatement, but since it must reduce its emissions by 90 per cent, its total expenditure is substantially greater than that of firm 2 for 10 per cent. While equity could support equal marginal costs, it might require that both firms spend the same amount, or abate by the same per cent. However, a requirement that each abate by fifty pounds would involve much greater total costs than requiring firm 1 to abate ninety and firm 2 to abate ten. In this case there is therefore a fundamental conflict between abatement efficiency and at least one definition of equity. This will be true in any case where the cost curves of firms are not identical. Except in cases of new plants producing the same product by similar technology and at the same scale it is reasonable to expect that there will be substantial variations in the costs of abatement from one firm to another.

So far we have discussed only the perfectly mixed case in which the marginal benefits of reducing each firm's emissions are the same. It should be recalled, however, that, in the more general case, in which the environment is not perfectly mixed, reducing emissions by one pound from one firm may have very different benefits from reducing emissions by one pound from another firm. If the benefits of abatement are very different for the various sources it is no longer sensible to equate marginal abatement costs. In the case of the river shown in Figure 2 the maximization of social welfare, which implies minimizing the sum of abatement costs from firms 1 and 2 and the damages to the beach, the fishing area, and firm 2, involves the solution of a complex mathematical algorithm. It would be entirely fortuitous if social welfare maximization in Figure 2 should involve equal marginal abatement costs for firms 1 and 2, equal percentage reductions, or equality in any other respect. Where pollutants are not perfectly mixed, so that each polluter's contribution to each pollutee's harm is not equal, no simple uniform policy can satisfy the criteria of social efficiency or abatement efficiency. This result has been well demonstrated by Johnson (1967), who found that a single effluent charge on a river did not even achieve the least-cost means of satisfying a single ambient water quality standard.

There is one situation besides the perfectly mixed case when abatement efficiency can be determined rather easily. Suppose that in Figure 2 there are no benefits from pollution control at the beach, the fishing area, or firm 2, but only at the mouth of the river, point B. Suppose, further, that firms 1 and 2 discharge the same pollutant, one that does not degrade or otherwise change in concentration as it moves down river. In this case, a one-pound discharge of pollutant by either firm will have an identical effect on water quality at point B. In short, the transfer coefficients a_1^B and a_2^B (as in equation 2.8) are identical. This case then becomes identical to the perfectly mixed case since the transfer coefficients are identical, so that equal marginal abatement costs will not only minimize total abatement costs but also best achieve social efficiency. If the pollutants are not conservative, however, or if all benefits do not occur downstream from the last polluter, the simplification can no longer be applied.

Thus the determination of who should clean up and how much is complex in most cases. Two criteria, social efficiency and abatement efficiency, must be applied. A dispersion model must be used to relate emission control to ambient quality. Finally, considerations of equity may conflict with either of the economic efficiency criteria. Only in simplified cases with perfect mixing or in the highly unrealistic stream case suggested above will a simple rule such as equal marginal costs satisfy even the abatement efficiency objective.

INTEGRATION OF ENVIRONMENTAL PROBLEMS

In the distant past, environmental problems tended to be viewed independently and their solutions approached on an isolated basis. If an apartment building had a solid waste problem reflected in high disposal costs for garbage, an incinerator might be installed. This would solve the solid waste problem by greatly reducing waste bulk and weight; the resulting air pollution might not be considered by the apartment operator if it were not illegal. When limestone scrubbing is used to remove sulphur dioxide from power plant stock gases, one by-product is a huge volume of limestone slurry, which is dried and placed into land fill or dumped into rivers where it can cause serious water pollution problems. When municipal sewage is treated at a sewage treatment plant, one by-product is sewage sludge, which may be used as fertilizer but is far more frequently burned or dumped at land fill sites. Many attempts to solve environmental problems have therefore inadvertently created other environmental problems.

One consequence has been the suggestion that all environmental problems are related. Partial analysis of individual environmental problems, it is suggested, will inevitably lead to error, and only global analysis of all problems together can result in policies assured of improving the environment. The debate has the familiar ring of that between those who advocate partial equilibrium analyses of individual economic problems and those who believe that anything short of a general equilibrium approach runs a serious risk of substantial errors. The Meadows and Meadows (1972) study for the Club of Rome may be regarded as the logical extreme of comprehensive treatment. Here, pollution problems are analysed simultaneously with population, food supply, and resource depletion.

The difficulty with this approach, which has been criticized by, among others, Roberts (1974), is that because of its very inclusiveness no component is very credible. The inclusion of many variables means that no variable is well defined; the inclusion of the entire world means that no area of the world is well represented. An aggregate pollution variable includes pollutants that may be easily controlled in the future. To this extent it must overstate the extent of a problem. Some pollutants may be discharged in areas where they cause no harm; their inclusion will again overstate the seriousness of the problem. The study is suspect because it tells more about mathematical functions involving exponential growth than it does about any aspect of the real world.

Less ambitious and more useful efforts have been made to integrate environmental analysis. Leontief (1971) has added to the traditional input-output table a row for pollution emissions and a column for pollution control. While this technique cannot evaluate costs and benefits of alternative control policies, it does permit estimation of future emissions from alternative mixes of final demand. It can be used to lay to rest the fear that producing pollution control equipment may in fact generate more pollution than is ultimately controlled by that equipment.

Another approach to integration of environmental analyses has been proposed by Kneese, Ayres, and D'Arge (1970). Their proposed material balance approach is really a way of ensuring that potential environmental problems are not overlooked. Starting from the principle of the conservation of matter, they note that everything that enters a production process must exit at some point. Materials included in the final product must have appeared as waste in some form or another. By subtracting final output from all inputs, they estimate residuals production and then examine all known discharges until these residuals can be accounted for. This does not help solve environmental problems, but it does help in identifying them.

Upon reflection it should be apparent that even partial analysis can be entirely satisfactory in the environmental field if sufficient thought is given to all the consequences of a given policy. For example, when regulation is proposed for a particular pollutant, thought should be given to the alternative means of disposing of that pollutant. Various control technologies should be examined to determine whether suppression of one pollutant will lead to an increase in another or will convert it to some other equally undesirable form. Where an increase in a technological external diseconomy can be anticipated as a result of controlling a given pollutant, a shadow price or penalty might be assigned to that externality. When marginal costs and benefits are compared the increase in the externality should be counted as a cost or subtracted from the benefits of the program. If this is carefully and properly done the partial analysis of the problem should include all environmental interactions and therefore be subject to no greater limitations than those apparent in any partial economic analysis.

A major advantage of partial analyses is that they are finite and feasible. It may be theoretically satisfying to conceive of evaluating all pollution problems at once, but it is rarely possible. If partial analyses are abandoned in favour of complete ones, no analysis can be completed in time for policy implementation. It is important to undertake analyses that can be completed in time to be of some use, and to look carefully, whether through material balance or other approaches, to insure that no significant undesirable side effect is ignored.

3
Benefits of pollution control

In the previous section a general framework for determining the optimal level of pollution was presented. This determination required that the marginal benefit of abatement be equated with the marginal cost. This chapter will consider the marginal benefit function, elements in that function, and various techniques for estimating them.

THE BENEFIT FUNCTION

The benefit of pollution abatement is the avoidance of pollution damage. If the damage caused by a certain level of air pollution in a city is X million dollars and that caused by a lower level is Y million dollars, then the benefit of abating by this amount is $X-Y$. We now proceed to classify and discuss the different types of damage done by pollution.

Classification and estimation of pollution damage
Ridker (1967) separates the effects of pollution into direct and indirect damages. Direct damage is harm inflicted by a pollutant upon persons or things with which it is in direct contact. For instance, if increased particulates contribute to an increase in the incidence of respiratory disease, if sulphur dioxide in the air increases the rate of corrosion of electrical contacts, or if the effluent dumped into a river by a municipality decreases dissolved oxygen and kills a species of fish, we can say that pollution has caused direct damage to some persons or things. It is difficult, however, to quantify even this direct relationship. In the health field, for instance, the influences of cigarette smoking, diet,

amount of exercise, and so on must be separated from those of pollution. This is often attempted with statistical techniques such as multiple regression analysis, but the exclusion of relevant variables or the use of a small data sample can lead to erroneous conclusions.

Controlled laboratory experiments are often used to determine the extent of effects such as fish loss or corrosion. Even when much is learned about the causal mechanism, however, it may be difficult to predict the degree of damage to objects under actual conditions. The rate of corrosion, for instance, depends on the humidity in the air and the physical configuration of the object as well as on the level of sulphur dioxide, and the damage to fish may depend on the temperature and turbidity as well as the dissolved oxygen concentration at a particular point. Such interactions between pollutants and other environmental conditions make it difficult to translate data which do not investigate these relationships into a schedule showing the physical damage caused by sulphur dioxide concentrations or dissolved oxygen levels in a particular air or watershed.

Further difficulties are encountered in evaluating the amount of economic damage. Decreasing the particulate level by 1 gram per 100 square metres per month may decrease the bronchitis mortality rate by 0.18 per cent, but what economic value can be placed on this? Fewer years of productive activity will be lost and smaller treatment costs incurred, but there will also be less suffering by the victims of this disease, a variable that is difficult to evaluate. A certain number of fish may be killed or their growth rate retarded, but what effect does this have on the sustainable yield of a fishery and what value can be placed on that yield? Even ascertaining the value of a given drop in yield can be a particularly contentious problem when the fishery involved is mainly recreational.

Indirect pollution damage is the cost of avoiding direct damage. It may be possible to avoid the harmful effects of air pollution by installing an air filtration system or by moving to a less polluted area. Metal may be coated with protective substances or more use made of corrosion-resistant metals. Actions will be taken by individuals to reduce pollution damage provided these measures cost less than the damage they prevent. The net impact is to reduce the harm done by pollution. But these measures are costly in themselves, and their cost should be added to the direct harm still incurred to get the total benefits of abatement.[1]

One problem in measuring adjustment costs is the difficulty of accounting for all the ways in which an individual may adjust to a given situation. A commercial

1 We might think of this adjustment process as analogous to the industry that decides to change its production process to a cleaner one rather than put some device on its stack. The added cost of transferring to and using the new production process is a cost of abatement.

establishment in a polluted area may hire additional maintenance personnel, put in an air filtration system, place protective coverings on inventories, tolerate more dirt than it otherwise would, and so on. In order to calculate the costs of avoidance one must be able to list all possible defensive actions, determine which ones are being implemented, and then calculate their cost. Furthermore, one must know not only the amount spent on damage avoidance but also how these expenditures will vary with the pollution level.

Both direct costs and costs of avoidance should be measured at their long-run values for long-run policy evaluation. Thus it may be that when pollution worsens in an area the direct damage incurred is very great, but as individuals have time to adjust to this higher level of pollution the direct costs will fall through damage avoidance measures and the costs of avoidance will rise. The total damages will then decrease from some high initial level to a stable long-run value. This chapter will focus primarily on long-run damage.

Adjustments of the type just discussed may result in costs or benefits to people not directly affected by the pollution because the economic effects are spread through the marketplace. These costs form Ridker's second type of indirect damage. An increased demand for corrosion-resistant metals will raise the price of these metals for all users, not just those directly affected by the pollution. Similarly, an increase in pollution in one area of a city will increase the value of houses in the less polluted areas. Sectoral shifts in demand may increase or decrease regional disparities in income and employment. These market effects are not true damages, however, since they result not only in losses to individuals such as the users of corrosion-resistant metals but also in offsetting gains to others, such as metals manufacturers. If markets work smoothly and costlessly, no added damages are created.

Such effects, however, do make it difficult to estimate the correct value of the adjustments to pollution since these are measured in terms of market prices that are already altered by the adjustment process itself. On the other hand, in some instances such as property value studies, they may provide a convenient way to measure the first two types of damage. It is important to avoid counting a particular kind of damage twice by adding market effects to direct costs or avoidance costs that the market effects themselves summarize.

Constructing an actual damage function requires consideration of pollution indices, relevant time periods, and dispersion models. The primary independent variable of a damage function will be some measure of air or water quality: grams per cubic metre of sulphur dioxide, parts per million of dissolved oxygen, and so forth. Unfortunately, choosing this measure is not a simple matter. What exists is a distribution of qualities over both time and space, but some number or set of numbers must be chosen to represent the whole distribution. Should we choose an average of daily or monthly observations, the minimum or maximum concentrations, or the mean as well as other moments of the distribution?

Theoretically it is best to use the measure most closely related to the damage. Often, however, this measure is not known. In his work on the effects of sulphates and particulates on mortality rates Lave (1972) found that minimum rather than maximum concentration is the most powerful measure, while an interview study in Nashville, Tennessee (Barrett and Waddell, 1973), indicated that an individual's perception of the pollution level was influenced more by the frequency of high daily levels of pollution than by high monthly, seasonal, or annual averages. Thus if two sections of a city have an equal number of days with high pollution levels per year but one section had more days with little or no pollution, the sections will still be regarded as equally polluted by the residents.

The time period considered is also important. The effects of a single severe pollution episode may be quite different from a similar pollution level over a longer period of time. The study of a severe pollution episode may overstate the costs of a sustained level of pollution because people will not have the same opportunities to adjust during the episode that they would have had if the level had persisted over a longer period. On the other hand, episodic studies may understate the level of damage since organisms may be able to recuperate from short exposures but not from long ones.

Any lags between the pollution level and the appearance of measurable effects must also be considered. Do the symptoms of a disease occur only after some period of exposure to pollution? Is the mortality or morbidity rate most influenced by the pollution levels of five years ago, this year, today, or perhaps the average level over the last twenty years? Decisions about the time period to be used, like those about the summary statistic for the distribution, should depend on the problem under consideration. In practice, however, the decision is often made on the basis of limited information.

The other independent variables chosen for the study must also be carefully considered. If a factor that causes damage to the item being studied is not included and if it is positively correlated with the pollution level, the coefficient of the pollution variable will be biased upward. A useful rule of thumb is that all factors having an influence at least as great as pollution must be considered. Since pollution is often a minor factor in the damage observed a great many other independent variables must therefore be used. This creates many statistical problems, the most formidable of which are the increased chance of multicollinearity and the large sample sizes needed to isolate the effects of different variables.

Finally, there is not a one-to-one relationship between ambient environmental quality and the emissions from all sources. A meteorological or hydrological model is needed to relate ambient quality to individual emissions. In such a model factors such as rainfall or wind direction are stochastic in nature. Thus even if all emissions are constant over time, they will result in a probability distribution of air quality, which in turn must be associated with some amount of damage.

This can be done by determining the probability that a certain state of the world, such as a particular level of stream-flow, will occur and multiplying this by the damages that would occur in this event. Summing products over all possible states of the world yields the value of the damage expected to result from a given amount of effluent. Frankel (1965) uses this technique to arrive at the benefits to downstream users of alternate degrees of sewage treatment by an upstream municipality.

Pollution abatement as a public good

Once we have determined the extent of physical damage caused by pollution and assigned an economic value to such damage, we must combine them in some manner to get the total damage caused by a given level of pollution. Pollution abatement or its result, a clean environment, is a public good. This means that the same ambient air or water quality affects each person it contacts. Persons in a small area must consume approximately equal environmental quality. We must therefore add the myriad damages caused by a given level of air or water quality to arrive at the total damages.[2]

This implies that the benefits of abatement depend on such factors as population density and the distribution of articles susceptible to damage. If decreasing air pollution reduces the morbidity rate for a disease by 1 per 10,000 population, then multiplying the change in morbidity rate by the population and dividing by ten thousand yields the number of man-days of disease avoided. Similarly, if a pollutant damages a type of plant that cannot be grown in the area under consideration, no damage of this kind has occurred.

Damage functions and the demand for a clean environment

Another way to see the damage function is as the demand for a clean environment. What would an individual be willing to pay for cleaner air or water? Obviously he would not be willing to pay more than the value of the damage he suffers from pollution. If each person could specify what he would be willing to

---

2 An extensive body of literature on the theory of public goods and their provision is applicable to the optimal provision of environmental quality. The basic articles in this field and the source of the definitions used here are Samuelson (1954) and (1955). An interesting extension of this theory directly applicable to pollution is Holterman (1972).

pay for each quality of air and water a schedule could be derived showing society's total willingness to pay for each degree of environmental quality. Once again, because all individuals can and must consume the same environmental quality the total willingness to pay would be the sum of the individual amounts.[3] This demand function would also be a benefit-of-abatement schedule.

Unfortunately such information is not readily available. Numerous questionnaires have attempted to determine what society is willing to pay for abatement (Ridker, 1967; Barrett and Waddell, 1973; Auld, 1973), but such studies are probably inherently doomed. Because one cannot exclude anyone from the environment it is impossible to organize a market in it, and people are therefore not accustomed to assigning a value to it. This is a problem for the questionnaire method of determining willingness to pay because individuals are notoriously poor at answering purely hypothetical questions. Furthermore, there is an incentive to mislead. If respondents suspect they may be charged the amount they say they are willing to pay, they may understate the amount to avoid being charged for a good from which they will benefit if the abatement is actually carried out. On the other hand, if they do not expect to be charged they may overstate the amount in the hope that a strong statement of concern will bring more action.

It may be, however, that an indirect-willingness-to-pay function can be constructed. People may be better able to say how much they would pay to carry on a given activity, such as swimming at a particular beach. If this amount changes when the quality of the water at the beach is improved they have indirectly expressed the value of this cleaner water. For society as a whole this would result in a shift in the willingness-to-pay schedule or demand function for swimming at the beach.

Figure 5 shows two hypothetical willingness-to-pay functions for such a beach. The lower curve DD shows the number of people who would swim at this beach for each hypothetical admission charge. The upper curve $D'D'$ is the same relationship but with cleaner water. The shaded area between the curves and above the actual admission charge A is the implied public willingness to pay for this improvement in water quality (Mäler, 1971).

Willingness-to-pay or demand functions and damage functions will be equivalent when the income effects of payment for quality improvement or compensation for the lack of it are small, when both damages and willingness to pay are accurately measured, and when people are fully aware of the effects of pollution

3 The concept of environmental 'quality' is actually a composite of many specific attributes and the specific change, both the initial and final states, must be clearly understood by all respondents in order for their answers to be comparable.

Figure 5
Benefit of a water quality improvement as determined by
a shift in the demand function for a beach

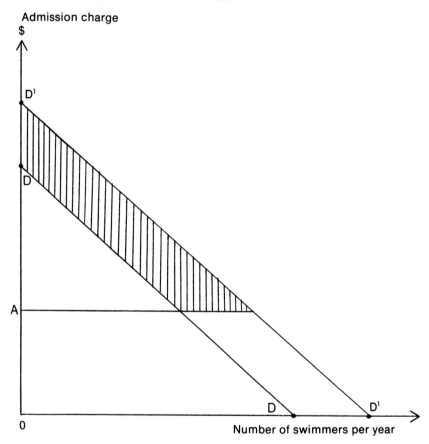

Admission charge

on them.[4] If, for instance, they are unaware that air pollution will increase their chances of contracting chronic bronchitis, or if they are unable to determine what a small increase in the small probability of contracting this disease means to them, they will not include this damage as one to be avoided when they state what they are willing to pay for pollution abatement. One may find that one

4 'Small' income effects are defined as changes in income that do not alter the marginal utility of money.

must estimate damage functions for cases like this where the effects of the pollution are not fully realized by the public and for willingness-to-pay functions when the damages are primarily aesthetic and thus can only be evaluated at their subjective worth to the individual.

Separable versus non-separable benefit functions
Whether one is trying to calculate a demand or a damage function another problem may arise: the function may be non-separable.[5] This can mean one of two things. First, the amount of damage may be a non-linear function of the quality of the environment. If so, the marginal benefits of abatement will depend on the initial level of pollution. Secondly, the various pollutants may interact in some way. They may combine with each other to form some new noxious substance, such as photochemical smog, or they may simply exacerbate the effects of one another. In such a case the benefit of abating all pollutants is not just the sum of the benefits of abating each pollutant taken separately.

Non-separable damage functions increase the amount of information required for policy-making. If damage functions are separable the marginal damage functions are horizontal lines that do not shift when the levels of other pollutants are changed. This means that if each producer is made responsible for the damages his effluents produce, optimal air or water quality will be achieved. If the function is not separable, however, the damage caused by a particular producer or pollutant cannot be uniquely defined since it depends on the actions of other producers and the levels of other pollutants. The damages caused by each producer as a function of the amounts of each type of pollutant he emits and the amounts produced by others can be combined with the costs of abatement to each producer. This whole system of equations must then be solved simultaneously to get the optimal levels of air or water quality and the optimal amount of abatement by each producer.

In the preceding section we mentioned several methods of arriving at pollution damage or abatement demand functions. These included measuring direct physical damage and assigning an appropriate value to it, using questionnaires to determine either directly or indirectly people's willingness to pay for environmental quality, and using the capitalization of pollution damage into the value of property as an estimate of the costs to affected individuals. In the following sections we will discuss some existing work on the construction of damage (or benefit) functions for air and water pollution and in the process illustrate each of the above methods more fully.

5 The concept of separability here is similar to that used when comparing separable and non-separable utility or production functions.

BENEFITS OF AIR POLLUTION CONTROL

If the amount of harmful substances in the air were reduced many benefits would be realized by a community. Homes, offices, and factories would require less cleaning, and less frequent painting. Clothing, automobile tires, and industrial machinery or consumer goods would last longer. Livestock and ornamental or commercial vegetation would be healthier and grow faster. The human population of the region would be ill less often and live longer. The community would be a better place to live in not only because of the reduction in these physical damages but because the aesthetic properties of the environment would be improved. In this section we will discuss in turn each of these physical benefits of abatement and then present a suggested method of measuring not only the physical damages avoided but the psychic ones as well.

Soiling and damage to materials

1 / Experimental evidence
All materials can be affected to some extent by air pollution. This damage may take a great variety of forms. Materials can be damaged by abrasion from the impact of wind-driven particles. They are subject to direct chemical attack, such as the tarnishing of silver or the etching of metals by acid mists, and indirect chemical attack, such as the deterioration of leather by absorbed sulphur dioxide, which changes to sulphuric acid in the leather.

One of the most important types of damage to materials is the electro-chemical corrosion of metals. Metallic surfaces have many anodes and cathodes created by local physical differences in the metal. In the presence of even a molecular layer of water on surfaces that appear dry a current will flow, permitting corrosion to take place. Because pollutants present in the air dissolve in the water and increase the conductivity of the film they increase the rate of corrosion.

Another very costly type of material damage is that caused by soiling and by the removal of soil. This may be reflected in an increase in cleaning frequency which, besides being costly itself, may increase wear on materials.

Table 1 shows the effects of pollutants on different types of materials. The information shown here is the result of carefully controlled laboratory studies which have pinpointed the direct effects as well as some of the interactions of pollutants. The synergistic effects of various pollutants may in fact be as important as their effects considered separately. It has been found, for instance, that sulphur dioxide causes much more rapid corrosion when combined with charcoal particles.

TABLE 1

Air pollution damage to various materials

Materials	Typical manifestation	Measurement	Principal air pollutant	Other environmental factors
Metals	Spoilage of surface, loss of metal, tarnishing	Weight gain of corrosion products, weight loss after removal of corrosion products, reduced physical strength, changed reflectivity or conductivity	SO_2, acid gases	Moisture, temperature
Building materials	Discolouration, leaching	Not usually measured quantitatively	SO_2, acid gases, sticky particulates	Moisture, freezing
Paint	Discolouration, softened finish	Not usually measured quantitatively	SO_2, H_2S, sticky particulates	Moisture, fungus
Leather	Powdered surface, weakening	Observation, loss of tensile strength	SO_2, acid gases	Physical wear
Paper	Embrittlement	Decreased folding resistance	SO_2, acid gases	Sunlight
Textiles	Reduced tensile strength, spotting	Reduced tensile strength, altered fluidity	SO_2, acid gases	Moisture, sunlight, fungus
Dyes	Fading	Fading by reflectance measurements	NO_2, oxidants, SO_2	Sunlight, moisture
Rubber	Cracking, weakening	Loss in elasticity, increase in depth of cracks when under tension	Oxidants, O_3	Sunlight
Ceramics	Changed surface appearance	Changed reflectance measurements	Acid gases	Moisture

SOURCE: Yocom and McCaldin, 1968, 624

These studies have also isolated some of the other factors that contribute to the amount of damage caused by a particular level of pollution. One of the most important factors is humidity. Experiments have shown that even highly polluted air causes little corrosion damage when the level of humidity is below 60 per cent. This is because the necessary water layers cannot be formed or maintained at these humidities. On the other hand, rain may decrease the amount of corrosion by washing the affected surfaces. High temperatures will increase the rate of chemical reactions, but low temperatures may result in the formation of dew that will increase the rate of electrochemical corrosion. Sunlight is necessary for the production of certain pollutants. For instance, the ultraviolet light in sunlight breaks nitrogen dioxide into nitrogen oxide plus atomic oxygen. The oxygen then combines with oxygen in the air to form ozone, one of the main ingredients of photochemical smog. Wind levels can determine the amount of abrasion as well as the dispersion and concentration of pollutants around a source. Even the position of a material in space can determine whether particulates impact upon it or settle on its horizontal surface; and, of course, the amount of damage can be controlled to some extent by protective measures such as painting or using more corrosion-resistant materials.

Although laboratory studies have contributed a great deal to our knowledge of the harmful effects of pollution, they have limitations for investigating the economic benefits of pollution abatement. As Table 1 shows, this damage is commonly measured by changes in weight, thickness, indexes of bending and tension, and fatigue or electrical resistance. What is important from the economist's point of view, however, is not that a metal plate gains or loses a few micrograms of weight in a controlled laboratory setting but that the useful life of a product is shortened or its efficiency reduced. We could measure economic loss only if we knew the added frequency at which a given item had to be replaced, cleaned, or serviced and the cost to the individual or firm of cleaning, replacing, or maintaining it. Expenditures to protect an item from the ravages of pollution should be added to the direct damages incurred.

2 / Total cost studies
Unfortunately many of the studies attempting to measure the economic cost of pollution have concentrated on estimating the total cost to a particular community of an existing level of air pollution, whereas what is needed is a function showing the amount of damage resulting from each of a range of different pollution levels. These studies generally calculate the total amount spent for a particular good or service and then make an educated guess about the portion of this expenditure that is the result of pollution.

For example, the Beaver Report (Great Britain, 1954) divided England into 'black' and 'clean' areas, with approximately one-half of the population living in the polluted sections. It then went on to state, 'The total consumers' expenditure on clothing and household textiles is not far short of £1,000 million a year. If the effect of air pollution is to reduce the life of textiles by one-tenth, on the assumption that one-half of the use of textiles is in polluted areas, then the cost will be of the order of £50 million a year' (ibid., 43). We can see that although this figure may provide some idea of the magnitude of the problem caused by pollution it is far from precise. We wish to know, not what percentage of an expenditure is caused by pollution, but how the total expenditure would change with different pollution levels. This would indicate the benefit of increasing the air quality by some marginal amount in a specific region.

Often the damage in this type of study is measured in terms of the frequency of performing some particular maintenance function. The Beaver committee obtained reports from local officials and evidence on the frequency of painting of two similar tracts of houses, one in an industrial area and one in the suburbs. It also received a report from a large chain store on the frequency of repainting its stores. These showed that buildings in polluted areas required repainting every three years, as opposed to every five years for buildings in 'clean' areas. The commission then made a 'conservative' estimate of four years as against six years, which resulted in a figure for additional expenditures in polluted areas of £3 per year for painting each house and £20 per year for painting each shop or warehouse. These figures, when multiplied by the number of houses and commercial establishments, showed an additional total cost of £26 million per annum for painting in England because of pollution (ibid., 41.2). Once again, we have only a measure of the savings from making a 'black' area 'clean,' not those of reducing pollution in an area with a specific initial air quality.

A study by Zerbe (1969) of air pollution in Canada, Ontario, and Toronto gives the kind of total-cost estimate discussed above. Zerbe estimated the percentage of expenditure due to pollution by using the Mellon Institute study of Pittsburgh (O'Connor, 1913), the Beaver report (Great Britain, 1954), Ridker (1967), and other sources and then estimated the total pollution cost to Canadians. He assumed that 64 per cent of the urban population in Canada lives in polluted areas. Thus Table 2 is only an indication of the general magnitude of the problem in Canada. It does give a conservative estimate of the benefit of removing all pollution and an idea of the areas where the most important benefits of abatement may be found, but it is of little help in making realistic policy decisions.

3 / Incremental expenditures approach
Many of the techniques first developed in this type of total-benefit study, however, can be adapted to derive a marginal benefit-of-abatement function. Ridker (1967), for example, tries a more sophisticated determination of the influence of

TABLE 2

Total pollution cost estimates for Canada, Ontario, and Toronto in 1965
(millions of Canadian dollars)

Category	Canada	Ontario	Toronto
1 House painting and repairing	137.70	65.66	25.06
2 Corrosion-inhibiting paint	2.10	1.02	0.40
3 Commercial and industrial painting and repairing	504.25	240.30	91.81
4 Stone and brick cleaning	13.72	6.43	2.32
5 Depreciation of buildings	11.95	5.81	2.20
6 Contract building maintenance service	26.40	12.58	4.81
7 Metal corrosion losses	20.84	31.00	9.07
8 Commercial and home and dry cleaning	68.63	32.63	17.53
9 Shelf goods	5.50	2.42	1.10
10 Clothing and furnishing	109.43	48.17	21.95
11 Mortality and morbidity	46.75	20.46	5.98
12 Rubber depreciation	4.29	2.08	0.79
13 Leather depreciation	0.65	0.32	0.12
14 Nursery plants	0.02	0.01	0.00
15 Air filtering equipment	0.33	0.16	0.06
16 Crops	6.23	1.05	–
17 Animals	1.78	0.78	0.23
18 Additional lighting	8.46	3.23	1.27
19 Additional transportation	7.71	3.37	0.99
Total	1,026.74	477.48	185.67
Per capita (dollars)	52.46	70.94	93.98

SOURCE: Zerbe, 1969

air pollution on expenditures for cleaning and maintenance. Like earlier studies, his concentrates on total expenditures in certain categories, but instead of trying to arrive at a percentage of those caused by air pollution he tries to explain total expenditures by the level of air pollution and other relevant factors. He also uses a continuous measure of air quality rather than simply dividing the area into polluted and unpolluted regions.

His first study compared laundry and dry-cleaning expenditures in cities with different levels of air pollution. The receipts of commercial establishments were run in a multiple regression with an index of suspended particulate matter, temperature, population, per capita income, and an index representing intercity price differentials. It is important that all of the variables other than the pollution index were included to account for their influence on the receipts. If it were true, for instance, that large industrial cities with high levels of air pollution also had higher prices than smaller less polluted cities, the effect of this price differential on differences in total receipts would have been erroneously attributed to air pollution had that variable been excluded. In order to avoid such a spurious correlation it is necessary to include all the factors other than air pollution that contribute to the differences in expenditure.

This study however showed no significant relationship between the amount of air pollution and the recipts of laundries and dry cleaners. A similar attempt to explain the cost of cleaning apartment buildings and office interiors in these cities adjusting for wage differentials and differences in climate also showed no significant relationship. Ridker points out that this might be because the single figure for the average particulate level at the measuring station in the city did not represent the true amount of air pollution over the whole city.

In an attempt to overcome the problem of the appropriateness of the pollution data in interurban studies, Ridker also attempted a number of intraurban studies for the St Louis area. Relatively good pollution data are available by area of this city. He attempted to measure the relationship between supermarket sales of cleaning supplies and the particulate level in different areas of the city. Only one supermarket chain responded to his request for data, a common problem of questionnaires. Here again he found no significant correlation. However, even with a better response he might have found none, since he arbitrarily defined market areas for each establishment, did not control for family income and ethnic factors that might influence cleanliness standards, and did not consider the possibility that consumers might simply tolerate more dirt or spend more time rather than more money on cleaning.

4 / Incremental frequency approach
Another technique that can easily be adapted from the total-cost studies is to compare the relative frequency with which certain cleaning tasks are performed. If the influence of air pollution on these frequencies can be isolated and a value put on the performance of the task, one can then infer the extra costs imposed by a particular level of air pollution.

Michelson and Tourin (1966) studied the relative frequencies with which certain household cleaning and personal care tasks were performed in the cities of Steubenville, Ohio, and Uniontown, Pennsylvania. These cities were chosen for their similarity in population and income level and difference in levels of pollution. Steubenville has an average pollution level of 383 micrograms per cubic metre, Uniontown 115. Unfortunately the two towns are quite different in other ways, such as occupational structures and local variance of air quality. But differences in the costs of cleaning and maintenance operations for the two towns were still attributed to the level of air pollution. This study therefore differs from the earlier total-cost studies only in considering two specific pollution levels and making some attempt through its choice of cities to hold other factors constant.

Survey response rates of 3 to 4 per cent in each town provided data on the frequency of the performance of certain tasks related to outside and inside maintenance of the home, to laundry and dry cleaning, and to women's hair and facial care. Income and educational levels of families and characteristics of the houses they occupied were gathered but were used merely to ascertain that the two samples were roughly equivalent in these respects. In the final study only two income categories were used to divide the sample into subgroups although more exact data had been collected.

Differences in the frequency with which the tasks were performed were transformed into economic costs using local commercial prices in the Steubenville area. This is an upper bound on the value of these services since a large number of families do not have these services provided commercially, implying that they can be done more cheaply by the individuals in the family. Hair and facial care values were measured at the price of the preparations used for these procedures. Obviously this is a lower bound on the value of these tasks since time and labour costs were neglected.

The results of this study are presented in Table 3. It can be seen that the cost to Steubenville of its level of pollution, or the benefit to it of achieving a pollution level of 115 micrograms per cubic metre, would be $3.1 million.

This study and another done by the same authors for the Washington area are the only ones indicating any relationship between material damage and/or soiling

TABLE 3

Summary of the economic cost of air pollution for home and personal care, Steubenville, Ohio, 1960

Activity	Gross cost differences (dollars)[a]	
	Annual	Per capita[b]
Outside maintenance of houses	640,000	$17
Inside maintenance of houses and apartments	1,190,000	32
Laundry and drycleaning	900,000	25
Hair and facial care	370,000	10
Total	3,100,000	$84

a Between Steubenville and Uniontown
b Based on estimated 1959 population of 36,400
SOURCE: Michelson and Tourin, 1966, 510

and the level of air pollution. Similar studies of the Philadelphia area by Ridker (1967) and by Booz-Allan and Hamilton (Barrett and Waddell, 1973) which included demographic data and information on attitudes towards cleaning showed no significant relationship between cleaning frequencies and the level of air pollution. Since both these studies were better designed to take account of factors other than air pollution that would influence cleaning frequencies, doubt is cast upon Michelson and Tourin's results. Despite the apparent flaws in the analysis their study has been used to justify certain abatement measures (Wilson and Minnotte, 1969). This highlights the importance of looking behind such cost-benefit studies as that done by Wilson and Minnotte to the sources of their benefit or cost data.

Studies of the cleaning and painting frequencies of commercial and industrial facilities have also confirmed the view that air pollution has relatively little effect on these frequencies. Using data supplied by a contract cleaning firm on the average, minimum, and maximum frequencies of performance of certain chores such as dusting fixtures and window sills, shampooing carpets, and so on for seven cities, Ridker has found that except for two tasks in one city all chores were performed with identical average, minimum, and maximum frequencies in all of the cities. Ridker comments that such results might be explained if cleanliness is judged by the frequency of cleaning and not by actual appearance or if modern office buildings that subscribe to cleaning services are relatively sealed off from the outside environment and thus not influenced as much as private homes by the ambient air quality.

In an intraurban study comparing similar businesses located in different parts of the city Ridker again found that most cleaning and maintenance was done on the same schedule regardless of the location of the establishment. This would simplify maintenance supervision; but if different levels of cleanliness really mattered to businessmen they would have sacrificed some of the savings of uniformity in scheduling for more uniformity in cleanliness. What individual differences existed could be explained by the type of parking lot around the building, the age of the building, how well it was sealed, and the type of air conditioning.

Finally, Ridker attempted to explain the frequency of painting of electrical transmission towers in the St Louis area which the electric company had stated were painted when 'necessary' rather than on a predetermined schedule. In a regression of the frequency of repainting versus a measure of dustfall, pollution seemed to have little effect. It could be, however, that this lack of explanatory power is the result of a poor correlation between pollution at the tower site and the measuring station, because other factors affecting the condition of the tower, such as wind velocity, were not adequately controlled for, or because other pollutants are more important than dustfall in determining painting needs.

5 / Conclusions

What does this mass of evidence, or non-evidence, mean? The lack of significant results in the studies cited here could mean that our measures of pollution are not sensitive enough to be useful in measuring such small differences in cost. Measures of particulates and dustfall may be particularly sensitive to the precise location of the measuring station, and the use of a single city-wide statistic is certainly inappropriate.

It could also mean that pollution is simply a minor factor compared with other causes of soiling and material damage. The fact that its influence on any given item is small, however, does not mean that its total significance is small, simply that this influence is very difficult to measure. When the small amount of damage observed is multiplied by the very large number of items affected, the over-all cost could still be great.

Damage to vegetation and livestock

There are three main problems in determining the extent of the economic damage to vegetation and livestock. First, it must be established that particular damage is caused by air pollution and not diseases, pests, or naturally occurring climatic conditions. Second, the degree of damage must be related to the quality of the air. Third, an economic value must be placed on this damage. Much progress has been made in recent years on the first problem, some on the second problem, but almost none on the third. We will review the evidence on each of these items in turn.

1 / Types of damage

Pollution harms both commercial and ornamental vegetation in a variety of ways. Dirt and soot may collect on leaves, inhibiting the passage of gases through the stomata; chemicals may affect the respiratory and osmotic processes; and polluted rains falling on the soil may kill necessary micro-organisms or destroy essential enzymes. Short exposures to high levels of pollution may scar the leaves and injure new growth. Although these damages result in characteristic patterns of injury, Hepting (1964) notes that "in four of the cases of forest tree damage recently either proven or considered likely to be caused by atmospheric constituents ... pathologists spent years eliminating other, more conventional possible causes.' The untrained observer may not even consider the possibility that damage is caused by air pollution. The loss of an ornamental tree or shrub, for instance, is seldom attributed to air pollution because the average homeowner is not trained to recognize the effects of various pollutants.

Prolonged exposure to low levels of pollution results in damages that are even harder to detect because of the lack of characteristic scarring. The reduced rate of growth or yield may not be detected even by trained agricultural agents until the reduction is very pronounced or widespread.

In the United States the pollutants that cause the most damage are, in decreasing order of importance, fluoride, ozone, sulphur dioxide, peroxyacylnitrates (PAN), and ethylene, with occasional damage caused by chlorides, chlorine, hydrogen sulphide, ammonia, various types of hydrocarbons, sulphuric acid aerosol, sulphates, and sulphites (Gillette, 1969). The pollutants that do the most damage in a particular area, however, are determined by the local industries, the automotive population, and local fuel use.

Among the first effects of pollution on vegetation to be identified and studied were those occurring in areas around metal smelters. Harmful effects from sulphur dioxide released by smelters in Sudbury and Wawa, Ontario, are well documented (Linzon, 1958, 1960; Katz, 1937, 1952; Gordon and Gorham, 1963; Dreisinger and McGovern, 1969; McGovern and Balsillie, 1973a, 1973b). Other isolated incidents of pollution damage have been documented around fertilizer plants (Crocker, 1969) and power stations (Hepting, 1964; Effer, 1972; US 1969c).

The best attempt to date to measure the extent and exact cause of pollution damage over a large area, however, was conducted by the Pennsylvania Department of Agriculture in 1969 (Barrett and Waddell, 1973). County agricultural agents were trained at a special workshop to detect pollution damage and were provided with forms to report pollution damage in their jurisdictions. The agents reported the type of damage, the suspected pollutant, the portion of each plant damaged, and the proportion of the plants in the crop affected. Expert help was provided where the agent was unsure of the cause of the damage and the injured parties were also asked to estimate the monetary loss incurred. The advantage of this type of approach is that existing manpower can be used to set up an extensive damage-monitoring network at a relatively low cost.

The main fault of the Pennsylvania study is that it made no attempt to correlate the observed injury with the ambient air quality that caused it. Studies of such effects are necessary in order to construct a damage function relating each level of air quality to a specific amount of damage. Most of the experimental work to date, however, has been aimed at identifying particularly resistant or susceptible plants and determining thresholds below which no visible damage occurs.

2 / Relationship between air quality and damage
Species of plants may differ greatly in their susceptibility to pollutants, and even within a species great genetic differences in resistance may occur. Furthermore, the amount of damage caused by a pollutant may depend on the temperature,

the amount of rainfall, and the time of its incidence in the growing season. Plants, for instance, are most susceptible during the months and at times of day when their photosynthetic rate is relatively high. Similarly, drought can make them more susceptible to injury by lowering plant resistance to various toxins. The duration of exposure is crucial. Investigators in Sudbury found that most sulphur dioxide injury to vegetation occurred when the level reached 0.95 ppm for one hour, 0.55 ppm for two hours, 0.35 ppm for four hours, or 0.25 ppm for eight hours (McGovern and Balsillie, 1973a).

It has been shown in Sudbury that the concentrations of heavy metals as well as sulphur and sulphate-sulphur in the soil and vegetation increases with proximity to the principal smelters and that the levels in soil and vegetation are correlated with the air quality (McGovern and Balsillie, 1973b). Furthermore, it has been shown that the rate of growth of plants decreases as the percentage of soil from the Sudbury area in their growing mixture is increased (Effers, 1972). Nevertheless, more study is needed, even in this area where extensive air quality monitoring and observation of damage has been undertaken, to establish a precise model of the relationship between air quality, soil quality, and vegetation damage.

3 / Economic losses

Of the information requirements mentioned earlier, determining the economic extent of the damage has received the least attention. We know, for instance, that in 1969 the Ontario Bean Producers' Marketing Board complained of bronzing to 50 per cent of the white bean crop in Kent county and damage in other counties in southern and western Ontario, presumably resulting from ozone from the Detroit-Windsor area. Furthermore, the average acreage devoted to beans in Kent county dropped from twenty thousand to ten thousand acres between 1966 and 1969 (Effers, 1972). The information that we need, however, is the market price of the beans destroyed each year after the ozone level had stabilized and the difference between the revenue from the beans which could have been produced on these lands in the absence of pollution and the revenue from the crops now produced. This assumes that the amount of land, labour, and other factors of production are held constant. The total value of the beans destroyed during years when the ozone level rose substantially would represent a short-run loss that could be reduced by switching to less susceptible crops and is thus relevant only to short-run, not long-run, policy-making.

In his study of the economic loss from damage to white pine in the Sudbury area Linzon (1971) has erred in using the market price of a product rather than the price net of production costs as a measure of economic loss. He used a careful tree-sampling program over a period of ten years to calculate that there is a net loss of 0.20 cubic feet per tree per year in a zone close to Sudbury as compared to a zone not affected by the smelter fumes. When this figure is combined with the number of white pines per acre, acres of forest, board feet of lumber per cubic foot of volume of the tree, and price per board foot of white pine, he finds a loss of $117,100 per year. But if there were an increased volume of wood available, additional men and machines would have to be used to harvest it, and this cost should be subtracted from the $117,000 figure to get the true net benefit to society.

Information is sometimes available from the records of court settlements and negotiated damage claims. In Dunnville, Ontario, between 1965 and 1967, cattle were injured when they grazed on lands exposed to fluoride emissions from a local fertilizer plant. The courts ordered over $270,000 in compensation payments for damages to plants and livestock during this period (Effers, 1972). In Sudbury, reports of investigations of injury to vegetation were turned over to the individuals harmed and the smelter responsible, and negotiation of damage claims was carried on between the two parties. If figures on these settlements were available they would provide some indication of the amount of economic damage.

Court data are always incomplete, however, because many law suits are settled out of court and consequently not included in such statistics. There is also no information on the method used by the court or the two negotiating parties to determine the value of the injury.

Failure to specify the method by which economic estimates are to be obtained is quite common. In the Pennsylvania study (Barrett and Waddell, 1973), for instance, the affected parties were asked to estimate the extent of their losses. The total damage reported was $11 million, including $7 million in loss of profits, $500,000 for reforestation, and $500,000 for grower relocation. No clear criteria for assessing the value of the loss were provided to the individuals, however, and thus these damage figures are extremely unreliable.

One study that has successfully dealt with the problem of assigning a value to agricultural losses due to pollution is Crocker's (1969) examination of the problem of damage to citrus groves and livestock in Polk County, Florida. Data on over six hundred sales of agricultural land was used in an attempt to determine the amount by which land values in polluted areas were reduced. Since the value of the land is the discounted value of the future profits of growing crops or raising livestock on it, differentials in land values should measure the losses from pollution.

Crocker found that citrus lands in the polluted area suffered an average reduction in price in 1961-2 of $150 per acre. By 1967, however, when it became apparent that the fertilizer plants would be forced to abate, this differential had disappeared. For grazing land he found that the price was actually four dollars per acre more in polluted areas. This was because the fertilizer plants had informally been given the choice of cleaning up their operations or buying the damaged land. Since lands used for citrus groves were more valuable in that use than as a dumping ground for waste fluorides, these lands were not purchased; but the grazing lands, less expensive than abatement, were being purchased by the fertilizer companies, thus driving up their price. Unfortunately this proper allocation of resources was disrupted in the sixties when the state passed emission standards for all fertilizer plants.

This successful use of the property-value method of determining the economic value of crop damage might be applied to an area such as Sudbury, where there is a great problem in determining the economic value of decreased forest or crop growth.

Health damage
One of the most important ways in which air pollution affects individuals is in their health. Air pollution has been shown to contribute to the incidence of certain respiratory diseases, and there is some evidence that it may also be related to the incidence of other diseases.

1 / Relationship of mortality and morbidity to air pollution
There are two measures of the frequency with which a disease occurs in a society: the morbidity rate, the number of people per unit of population who contract a given disease during a period of time, and the mortality rate, the number of people per unit of population who die from a given disease during a period of time. Each expresses the probability that an individual in a population will contract or die from the disease in a given year. These rates may be calculated for the population of a country, region, or category of individuals (e.g. men between the ages of thirty-five and forty, smokers, those who are over five pounds overweight, and so forth). If these rates vary systematically with the level of air pollution to which the population is exposed one might conclude that air pollution is a contributory cause of the disease.

Two types of study relate these rates to the level of air pollution. The first type is primarily concerned with the change in mortality rates during severe pollution episodes. Such severe incidents have occurred and been studied in London, Yokohama, Donora (Pennsylvania), New York City, and elsewhere (US 1969c). We will not discuss the results of any of these studies for several reasons. First, they deal with the effects of short-term exposure to a very high level of pollution and the results obtained cannot be immediately translated into the effects of the same levels of pollution over a longer period of time both because the human body may be able to recover from a very short-term exposure and because people do not have the same opportunities for adjustment that they would have over a longer period. Secondly, those who die during such incidents are primarily those who are already critically ill. No light is shed on the causes of already existing illnesses or the extent to which the normal pollution level has contributed to them. Furthermore, it is difficult to place an economic value on the life of someone who is about to die and who has little chance of ever again being a productive member of society.

Lave and Seskin (1970) have written an excellent article summarizing studies that relate the long-term level of air pollution with mortality rates from respiratory and cardiovascular diseases. All the studies they report on suffer from a number of common problems. For one thing, the investigators cannot be sure that the death certificates accurately list the causes of death. Especially for a disease such as chronic bronchitis, which was not considered to be a major killer until quite recently, the cause of death given on a death certificate may be wrong. Furthermore, the certificates may be less accurate in rural areas, which are often compared with more polluted cities. Where the persons conducting the study actually performed autopsies the sample sizes were too small to yield conclusive results.

Another problem was the lack of correction for other factors that influence mortality rates from these diseases, such as age, smoking, occupational exposure, personal exercise and dietary habits, and genetic background. All of the studies reported held at least one of these factors constant, but none, except that by Lave and Seskin, held more than two of them constant.

A number of studies compared differences in mortality rates, adjusted for age and smoking, in urban and rural areas. Although this procedure may provide evidence that air pollution was implicated as a cause of the disease in question, it does not help to construct a schedule relating the level of pollution to the incidence of the disease. Other studies, although they included a more precise measure of air pollution, corrected the data only for persons per acre or, in some cases, social class.

The best study, Lave and Seskin (1972), compares total and infant mortality rates for 114 standard metropolitan statistical areas in the United States with a measure of the minimum concentration of either suspended particulates or total sulphates in micrograms per cubic metre. The results of their study are presented in Table 4. They show that a 10 per cent decrease in the minimum concentration of measured particulates would decrease the total death rate by 0.5 per cent, the infant death rate by 0.7 per cent, the neonatal death rate by 0.6 per cent, and the fetal death rate by 0.9 per cent.

These results hold the number of people per square mile constant as well as partitioning the population according to whether an individual is non-white, over sixty-five, or poor. A number of alternate specifications of the equation were

TABLE 4

Regressions relating infant and total mortality rates to air pollution and other factors in 114 standard metropolitan statistical areas in the United States

| Category | R^2 | Air pollution (minimum concentrations) | Persons per square mile | Socioeconomic | | |
				Percentage non-white	Percentage over 65	Percentage poor
Total death rate						
Particulates	0.804	0.102	0.001	0.032	0.682	0.013
		(2.83)	(2.58)	(3.41)	(18.37)	(0.93)
Sulphates	0.813	0.085	0.001	0.033	0.652	0.006
		(3.73)	(1.86)	(3.56)	(17.60)	(0.49)
Death rate for infants of less than 1 year						
Particulates	0.545	0.393		0.190		0.150
		(3.07)		(6.63)		(3.28)
Sulphates	0.522	0.150		0.200		0.123
		(1.91)		(6.83)		(2.70)
Death rate for infants less than 28 days old						
Particulates	0.260	0.273		0.089		0.063
		(2.48)		(3.61)		(1.60)
Sulphates	0.263	0.170		0.097		0.047
		(2.57)		(3.96)		(1.23)
Fetal death rate						
Particulates	0.434	0.274	0.004	0.171		0.106
		(2.02)	(2.01)	(5.70)		(2.11)
Sulphates	0.434	0.171	0.004	0.181		0.085
		(1.95)	(1.82)	(5.87)		(1.71)

NOTE: Values in parentheses are the *t*-statistic.
SOURCE: Lave and Seskin, 1970

tried to determine the form that best fit the data and separate regressions were run for males and females. The fact that the separate male and female equations showed almost identical influences of pollution indicates that occupational exposure is not a significant factor in death from these causes.

2 / Economic losses

Once the level of air pollution has been related to the mortality or morbidity rate, the next task is to assign some value to these deaths or illnesses. To evaluate a change in the mortality rate one must first use an age or other category-specific mortality rate and multiply the change in it by the number of people in that category to determine the number of additional people who will die each year of the disease. Then one must place a value on each of these deaths.

Ridker (1967) suggests that this value can best be approximated by the present value of the future earnings of the individual plus the savings from the delay of his burial. The present value of the probable future earnings of an individual who is a years old is

$$PV_a = \sum_{n=a}^{\infty} \left[\frac{P_{a_1}{}^n \cdot P_{a_2}{}^n \cdot P_{a_3}{}^n \cdot Y_n}{(1+r)^{n-a}} \right],$$

where $P_{a_1}{}^n$ is the probability that an individual will live to age n, $P_{a_2}{}^n$ is the probability that an individual living at age n will be in the labour force, $P_{a_3}{}^n$ is the probability that the person in the labour force will be employed, Y_n is the average annual earnings for workers of age n, and r is the appropriate discount rate. One of the main problems that arises here is the valuation of those who are not in the labour force but who do productive work. This category consists primarily of women working in the home but it may include any individual who receives part of his income in kind.

The second cost saved if the individual does not die is the cost of burial. Everyone must die eventually, of course, so this is merely a saving from delaying the time of burial. For an individual of age a it is equal to

$$C_a = C_0 \left[1 - \sum_{n=a}^{\infty} \left(\frac{P_a{}^n}{(1+r)^{n-a}} \right) \right],$$

where C_a is the present value of the delay of burial, C_0 is the cost of burial, P_a^n is the probability that an individual will die at age n, and r is the appropriate discount rate.

If we are dealing with morbidity rather than mortality statistics, we must determine the cost, to each person who contracts the disease, of professional care (doctors' visits, nursing services, the use of special facilities, and the like) and medications. This is fairly easy to do if the disease requires hospitalization but more difficult when the patient is treated at home. In this case the nursing services provided by some other member of the family are often valued at what they would cost if provided in a hospital. Such a valuation is almost surely an overstatement of true costs because of the lesser training of the person doing the home nursing and the absence of the extensive medical support facilities provided by the hospital.

To the professional care and medication costs must be added the value of the wages forgone in order to find the cost of the disease. This requires knowledge of the average duration of the illness and the average wage of the individual in this category. And this assumes that the individual's contribution to production is equal to his wage and neglects the effect that his absence may have on the efficiency of his fellow workers.

In all of these considerations we have not mentioned the pain and suffering caused by a disease. Even if a person were fully compensated for his lost wages and treatment costs, he would probably still choose not to have the disease. It is very difficult to measure this suffering. It would certainly be difficult for an individual to say how much he would be willing to pay for a small reduction in the probability of an improbable event such as contracting the disease. Mishan (1971a) asserts that however difficult such estimation may be it is the only approach consistent with the basic tenets of cost-benefit analysis. It has been suggested (Schelling, 1968) that one could arrive at a subjective value of human life by looking at expenditures by which individuals attempt to alter the probability of death, such as the purchase and use of safety equipment in an automobile. A cursory look at these statistics, however, shows a marked discrepancy in the value placed on human life under different circumstances.

Most of the existing estimates of the health damages caused by pollution are framed in terms of the total cost for the existing level of pollution (Bates, 1972; Zerbe, 1969). Even Lave and Seskin (1970), who conducted the most sophisticated study of the relationship of pollution and mortality rates, can only state that it appears that air pollution is responsible for about 20 per cent of respiratory and cardiovascular disease and then use a figure for the total cost due to these diseases in the United States to determine the loss per year from air pollution at current levels. All of the criticisms of total cost studies in the material damage and soiling section apply equally well here.

Property-value method of measuring damages
One way of estimating the cost of air pollution is through a study of its influence on housing prices. Since the effects of air pollution are location-specific and the supply of housing in each location is fixed in the short run, the harmful effects of the pollution will be capitalized into the price of a house; that is, if people have full knowledge of the effects of pollution on them and their property and they are able to place a monetary value on these damages, they will be willing to offer a price for a property in a cleaner area that exceeds the price they would offer for a similar house in a dirty area by the present value of the damages avoided.

Unfortunately, the market does not give us information about the offer prices of all individuals for all houses. What we know are the actual market prices of the houses. The differential between the prices of identical houses in areas that differ only in their amount of pollution is the market-clearing price for clean air.

Figure 6
The relationship between the property valuation function
and willingness to pay for air quality

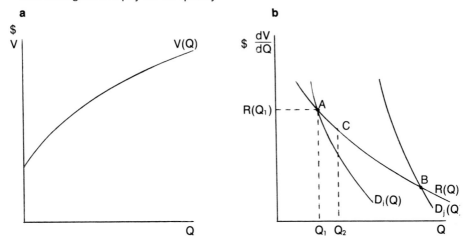

Figure 6a, from Freeman (1974), shows the observed value of a house V as a function of the air quality Q at its site. In Figure 6b, $R(Q)$ is the marginal purchase price of air quality. If a person is presently occupying a house with air quality Q_1, he must pay $R(Q_1)$ dollars more for a house with marginally better air quality. $D_i(Q)$ and $D_j(Q)$ are the demand curves for clean air of individuals i and j. Since utility maximization requires that each individual set $D_i(Q) = V'(Q_i) \equiv R(Q_i)$, the slope $R(Q)$ of the property-value function $V(Q)$ is actually the locus of the equilibrium marginal willingness-to-pay of all households. Only if the demand curves of all individuals are identical (sufficient conditions for which are identical utility functions and incomes) will $R(Q)$ itself be an individual's demand curve.

These points can be illustrated if we postulate two sets of houses identical in every way except for being located in areas with different air qualities. To simplify further, assume that we have a set of families equal to the number of houses and that each family will buy one house. Their choice then is simply one of which area to live in. The number of families wanting to buy houses in each area is a function of the price of houses in that area, the price of houses in the other area, the amount of pollution in each area, and the prices of all other goods and services the families would be willing to give up in order to have clean air.

Such a situation is pictured in Figure 7 where OQ_d is the supply of houses in the dirty area and OQ_c the supply in the clean area. P_d and P_c are the prices for

Figure 7
Equilibrium price differential for houses in different regions

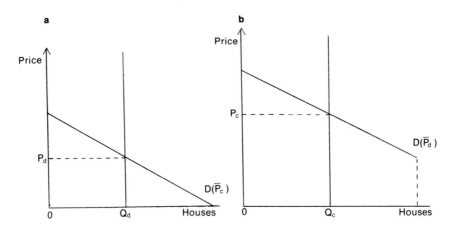

these types of houses respectively. $D(\bar{P}_c)$ and $D(\bar{P}_d)$ are the demand curves consistent with these prevailing prices. Now, there exists on the margin at least one person who is just indifferent between living in the dirtier area and paying more for a house in the cleaner area. For him, the value of the damage done by pollution is exactly equal to the price differential. Since it appears to each individual that he may choose either to stay in the dirtier area or to move to the cleaner area, the pollution damage to people who stay in the dirty area must be worth less to them than the price differential. This differential, multiplied by the number of houses in the dirty area, is an upper bound on the difference between the pollution damage in the two areas. In terms of Figure 6, this is equivalent to approximating the benefits to i of abating an amount Q_2-Q_1 by the area ACQ_2Q_1. Benefit estimates using this method become poorer as larger changes in air quality are considered.

This is not to say that if the level of pollution were reduced to that of the cleaner area tha value of the houses in the dirty area would increase by the amount of the differential. If, for instance, we reduced the pollution in one-half of the dirty area so that these houses were identical to the houses in the clean area as is shown in Figure 8, the price of the houses in the clean area would initially fall to P_c'' because of the added supply of this type of house, and the price of the polluted houses would rise to P_d''. After the demand curves had

Figure 8
Change in the equilibrium price differential for houses
when abatement takes place

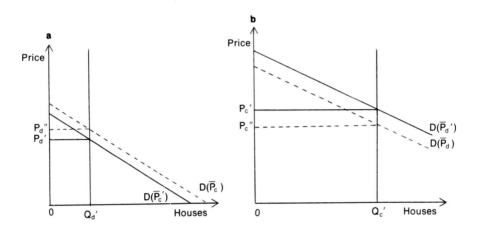

adjusted to the new prices in the submarkets, however, an equilibrium would be
reached with prices P_d' and P_c'. Once again the new differential multiplied by
the number of houses in the dirty area OQ_d' would be an upper bound on the
damage. We cannot tell by what amount the prices of the houses will change or
the exact amount of the new differential without a general equilibrium model
that specifies not only the reactions of individuals to various price differentials
and amounts of pollution but their tradeoffs between the amount of housing
services the amount of other types of goods and services they will buy as a
function of the quality of the housing and their incomes.

Scarth (1973) has suggested a method by which, with certain assumptions
about the form of the common utility function, one might estimate the change
in the value of a house caused by a change in pollution level. Even if one could
accurately predict these changes, however, this would not be a benefit-of-
abatement function except under certain assumptions about the intercity
mobility of individuals (Polinsky, 1973; Polinsky and Rubinfeld, 1975; US
Senate, 1974). The net increase in all property values, both residential and
commercial, would be the benefit of abatement to landowners, but unless the
utility level of individuals is fixed by an influx or exodus of individuals to
eliminate any intercity differentials in utility the increase in utility to individuals
must be added to the increase in property values.

TABLE 5

Summary of property value study results

Authors	Ridker and Henning	Anderson and Crocker
City	St Louis	St Louis
Year	1960	1960
Dependent variable	Mean property value for owner-occupied single	
Independent variables		
Constant	−2800	3.5407(0.63)
Pollution	index annual geometric mean sulphation, 1963-64 −245.0(88.1)	mean sulphur oxides −0.1019(0.03)[b] mean suspended particulates −0.1192(0.05)[b]
Neighbourhood characteristics		
Density		
rooms per unit	488.5(41.1)	
persons per unit	−3210(548.7)	
houses per mile (HPM)	116.6(20.4)[c]	
Quality of houses (%)		
recently built	48.36(7.20)	
old		−0.0257(0.02)[b]
dilapidated		−0.0802(0.990)[b]
Occupational homegeneity (OCC)	16940.0(2840.0)[d]	
Ethnic (%)		
non-white (PNW)	0.1961(0.0623)[e]	0.0373(0.006)[b]
Italian		
Ukrainian		
Jewish		
Distance		
to central business district (DIS)	320.2(138.7)[f]	−0.1387(0.04)[b]
highway access	922.5(278.9)	
Public services		
school quality	398.2(302.2)	
crime rate		
Illinois or Missouri	−819.8(369.1)[a]	
Mean family income	0.9374(0.1057)[a]	0.7660(0.08)[b]
R^2	0.937	0.7550
SEE		0.0311

NOTE: standard errors in parentheses in Ridker and Henning and in Anderson and Crocker; *t*-statistics in parentheses in Zerbe

a Residualized	*c* $(HPM - 2.42)^2$	*e* $(PNW + 14)^2$
b Natural logarithm	*d* $(OCC - 0.64)^2$	*f* $(DIS - 3.82)^2$

SOURCES: Ridker and Henning, 1967, 254; Anderson and Crocker, 1971a, 175; Zerbe, 1969, 46-52, 56-9

TABLE 5 cont'd

Anderson and Crocker		Zerbe	
Washington DC 1960	Kansas City 1960	Toronto 1961	Hamilton 1961
family houses			
3.3901(0.40)	3.5775(0.73)	−2557.58	3692.10
−0.0712(0.02)[b]	−0.0782(0.04)[b]	index: mean SO_2 1961-67	SO_2, 3-category
−0.0610(0.03)[b]	−0.0876(0.04)[b]	−966.29(2.16)	−579.94(2.28)
		5535.45(366.13) −3717.73(150.96) −0.29(9.34)[a]	2117.16(33.24)
−0.0106(0.01)[b] 0.0044(0.006)[b]	−0.0721(0.0124)[b] −0.0405(0.990)[b]	12.23(4.70)	9.62(2.20)
		83.04(27.86)	−163.76(61.24)
0.0251(0.006)[b]	0.0058(0.007)[b]	88.63(36.86) 143.57(9.61) 85.51(59.64)	191.07(5.13)
−0.0582(0.0158)[b]	−0.0623(0.02)[b]	−49.75(2.94)	355.60(2.90)
		8.33(2.59)	
0.7677(0.04)[b]	0.6720(0.09)[b]	2.70(124.0)[a]	
0.6966 0.0222	0.8231 0.0241	0.958 1510.35	0.97 638.52

A multiple regression analysis can determine the price differential of houses due to the pollution level where houses are not all identical except for this factor. The price of a house is explained by characteristics of the property, such as the number of rooms in the house or the acreage of the lot, and of the neighborhood in which it is located, such as the pollution level, the quality of public services, or the travel time to the central business district. Ridker and Henning (1967), Anderson and Crocker (1971), and Zerbe (1969) have all made similar studies of the effects of air quality upon housing prices. The preferred results of these three studies are shown in Table 5.

There is still some debate about whether or not the income level of the occupant should be included in this regression (Ridker and Henning, 1967; Nourse, 1967; Freeman, 1971; Anderson and Crocker, 1971). Although the final price of each house depends upon the alignment of houses of different quality with the number of people in each income level, this income level is held constant in a cross-sectional analysis. Therefore it would seem to be inappropriate to include it in the regression; characteristics of the house only, not of its owner, should be used. If income were to be used as an independent variable in the regression and the premium paid for clean air rose with the level of income, we would observe that the houses in the cleaner areas would be owned by those with higher incomes. The income variable would tend to pick up all this effect even though the higher-income people lived in these houses because they were cleaner.

Ridker and Henning and Zerbe use mean family income (MFI) for a census tract as a neighborhood characteristic, but they residualize it to avoid the problem mentioned above. With this technique, one first runs the regression

$$MFI = a_1 + a_2 \text{ Pollution} + \epsilon.$$

One then uses the residuals ϵ as a new variable RMFI in the main regression. This has the effect of attributing all of the covariance between pollution and the mean family income to the pollution variable. This technique is also used to alleviate some of the severe problems of multicollinearity between pollution and other variables faced in all three studies. A number of equations can be run in which the covariance is first attributed to the pollution variable and then to the other variable, giving an upper and lower bound on the pollution coefficient.

Ridker shows that for the St Louis area a drop in exposure by 0.25 mg of $SO_3/100cm^2/day$ would decrease the damage to the householder by about \$245. Anderson and Crocker find that a reduction in exposure of 10 micrograms/m^3/day of suspended particulates and 0.1 mg $SO_3/100cm^2/day$ sulphation would avoid damage of between \$300 and \$700 per property. Zerbe finds that reducing his sulphation index by one unit would avoid damages of $966 per household in Toronto and $882 in Hamilton.

The final question in these studies is: exactly what is being discounted by the property owners? The model introduced earlier in this section hypothesized that individuals had perfect knowledge of all the myriad ways in which pollution affects them. But that is obviously not the case. If, for instance, a potential homebuyer is unaware that his house will need more frequent repainting but is aware that the pollution cuts down the view he will not discount the first type of damage into the value of the property but will discount the second. If he were including all damages in his calculations the housing price differential alone could be used to determine a damage function, but if there are damages he is not taking into account they must be added to those shown in the price differential.

Little is known, however, about the amount of knowledge buyers possess. The best that can currently be done is to separate the housing market into submarkets, like owner-occupied dwellings or industrial facilities, on the ground that the buyers in these submarkets possess different amounts and types of information, and then make a careful guess about what damages are being discounted in each of the submarkets.

BENEFITS OF WATER POLLUTION CONTROL

One of the most fruitful ways of viewing many types of water pollution damage is that it is at most the cost of total avoidance of the damage, that is, the cost of treating the water to make it suitable for a given use. If it is not optimal to treat water to this level, the damage it is known to cause must be less than the cost of treatment.

Consider the case of the recent discovery of carcinogens in the drinking water of some United States cities for example. Although the presence of these agents may have caused much loss of life in the past, the maximum loss that should be considered in a forward-looking public policy is the cost of totally removing them from the drinking water. If such a procedure were followed there would be no further damage to public health, but the treatment costs would have to be included as pollution damage. One might decide to treat the water to reduce the level of carcinogens only to some 'safe' level if one found that further treatment would be more costly than the public health injury resulting from the presence of minute amounts of these substances. In such a case the cost estimate for the *total* elimination of the substances would be an overestimate of the damage. One would, of course, have to know the cost of total removal for each initial water quality in order to calculate a marginal benefit function that could be compared with the marginal cost of abatement at the source of the pollution.

Domestic and industrial use

Domestic and industrial use of water is very important in Ontario. Approximately 16,000 million gallons of water are pumped from the Great Lakes daily by 240 communities. This water is used for both domestic consumption and industrial use where the firm is connected to the municipal water supply. In addition, it is estimated that three times this amount is pumped for industrial use and not channeled through municipal supply systems.

Looking at domestic water use we would want to know the incremental cost of treating water of various qualities to the point where it is fit for human consumption. Young, Popowchak, and Burke (1965) have calculated the relationship between chemical costs per thousand gallons treated and nine measures of water quality (BOD, COD, hardness, colour scale, DO deficit, total dissolved solids, C1 demand, C1, and turbidity) for fourteen cities. The results of their regressions are shown in Table 6. One problem was that high multicollinearity between the different quality measures made their coefficients change greatly when different variables were used. They also had few observations on which to base their cost curves and could not adjust for other factors that might influence chemical costs such as the size of the treatment facility. Nevertheless, their results indicate that in most cases the additional chemical costs are quite small. In no case does a one unit increase or decrease in the quality measure result in a change of over one cent per thousand gallons of water treated.[6]

Frankel (1965) has calculated the incremental cost imposed on a downstream municipality by the discharge of sewage treated to various extents by an upstream municipality. Using a hydrological model of the Eel River in California and considering different amounts of discharges and intakes by the two cities he compares the cost of treatment of the drinking water as compared to the cost of treatment of the sewage water. Table 7 presents his findings on the incremental annual cost imposed on the downstream user by the discharge of wastes treated to two different levels for different initial conditions of the stream. He finds that in order to justify abatement upstream on the basis of the cost savings downstream alone, the downstream city would have to withdraw from sixteen to 250 times as much water as the upstream user was discharging. This ratio depends on the types of treatment plant being considered, the distance between the polluter and the water intake, and the initial quality of the stream.

The quality of water necessary for industrial use depends on the particular process for which it is to be used. Table 8, showing water quality criteria for use

6 The standard water quality criteria considered here do not include mercury, asbestos, or complex organic compounds that may prove to be harmful, even in minute quantities, when exposure occurs over a long time. Neither the damages caused by these substances not the treatment methods for their removal have been studied enough to warrant inclusion here.

TABLE 6

Cost equations for water treatment

Independent variable	Cost equation	$\bar{R}$	$2S_E$
Single-variable correlations			
BOD, ppm	$C = -0.31 + 0.784[X]$	0.87	0.86
Hardness, ppm	$C = -0.49 + 0.031[X]$	0.79	1.28
Colour, units	$C = \ \ \ 0.31 + 0.074[X]$	0.93	0.74
COD, ppm	$C = \ \ \ 0.10 + 0.072[X]$	0.87	0.90
DO deficit, ppm	$C = \ \ \ 0.14 + 0.10[X]$	0.92	0.64
Log TDS, ppm	$C = -4.66 + 2.56[X]$	0.71	1.13
Multiple variable correlations			
BOD, ppm Hardness, ppm	$C = -0.63 + 0.2357[BOD] + 0.0112[H]$	0.77	1.30
BOD, ppm Hardness, ppm Turbidity, units	$C = -0.89 + 0.2948[BOD] + 0.0137[H]$ $-0.0011[T]$	0.80	1.23
BOD, ppm Hardness, ppm Turbidity, units Colour, units	$C = -0.302 + 0.02400[BOD] +$ $0.00600[H] -0.00014[T] +$ $0.05554[Colour]$	0.97	0.49
Hardness, ppm Colour, units	$C = -0.24 + 0.0055[H] +$ $0.0574[Colour]$	0.98	0.45
Hardness, ppm COD, ppm	$C = \ \ \ 0.09 + 0.00625[H] + 0.0169[COD]$	0.66	1.27

NOTE: C is cost in cents per thousand gallons; X is independent variable
SOURCE: Young, Popowchak, and Burke, 1965, 294-5

in the leather tanning and finishing industry, illustrates the diversity of requirements even within an industry. The most troublesome characteristic of water
from the viewpoint of the industrial user is its hardness. This is usually the result
of natural factors rather than pollution. Most processes can tolerate quite a large
range of other characteristics of the water, and uses that are highly sensitive to
water quality, such as pressure boiler feed water, require special treatment of
even the best quality water occurring naturally. These treatment costs do not
vary greatly with the quality of the original intake water.

Damage to aquatic life
Water pollution is harmful to aquatic life in one of two ways. Toxic substances
or the lack of dissolved oxygen content in the water can reduce the ability of the
organisms to live and reproduce, or substances may be ingested by the organisms

TABLE 7

Comparison of total annual costs imposed on water treatment operation by disposal of domestic wastes upstream

	Raw waste discharge upstream				Trickling filter effluent discharge upstream			
Stream condition	5 mi	10 mi	20 mi	50 mi	5 mi	10 mi	20 mi	50 mi
Previously clean stream	980	840	760	520	540	490	430	410
Previously polluted stream plus domestic waste	2080	2020	1750	1510	1690	1670	1420	1340
Previously polluted stream	1490	1390	1280	1060	1060	1040	960	880
Incremental cost of additional pollution load	590	630	470	450	630	630	460	460

NOTE: Additional annual costs of water treatment operation ($/mgd), based on a 2.5-mgd water treatment plant.
SOURCE: Frankel, 1965, 179

TABLE 8

Water quality criteria for the leather tanning and finishing industry

Characteristic	Tanning process	General finishing processes	Colouring
Alkalinity (CaCO$_3$)	a	130	130
pH, units	6.0-8.0	6.0-8.0	6.0-8.0
Hardness (CaCO$_3$)	150	b	c, d
Calcium (Ca)	60	b	c, d
Chloride (Cl)	250	250	e
Sulphate (SO$_4$)	250	250	e
Iron (Fe)	0.3	0.3	0.1
Manganese (Mn)	0.2	0.2	0.01
Organics: Carbon chloroform extract (CCE)	e	0.2	c
Colour, units	5	5	5
Coliform bacteria, count/100 ml	f	f	e
Turbidity	c	c	c

NOTE: units are mg/1 unless otherwise stated
a Accepted as received if meeting total solids or other limiting values
b Lime-softened
c Zero, not detectable by test
d Demineralized or distilled water
e Concentration not known
f OWRC drinking water objectives
SOURCE: Ontario, 1973c

which, although not causing much damage to the organisms themselves, enter the food chain and prevent the fish from being used for human consumption.

Much work has been done in laboratories to determine the reactions of fish to various types of water quality. We know, for instance, that turbid water causes the gills of fish to become clogged with silt, increasing coughing and decreasing their respiratory efficiency. Low dissolved oxygen content in water causes them to increase both the rate and depth of respiration and also to become more active. The latter characteristic has the fortunate consequence that it often removes the fish from toxic waters if these areas are small enough.

Despite a great deal of laboratory study we know little about the effect of water quality on the population dynamics of various species under actual conditions. In one of the earliest field studies, for example, Ellis found that streams with 5 ppm dissolved oxygen seemed to support an active and varied fish population whereas those with less than this level did not (Jones, 1964). Laboratory studies, however, have shown that fish are able to survive dissolved oxygen levels far below standard. The explanation for this, of course, is that there is quite a difference between surviving temporarily and being able to live indefinitely while feeding, growing, reproducing, and competing with ones enemies.

Figure 9 depicts a relationship between the oxygen content of water and the ability of fish to function. The incipient lethal standard is that found in the laboratory to maintain life without excess activity, including feeding. An active fish naturally requires a much higher oxygen consumption rate. The difference between the minimum oxygen consumption rate necessary for life and the level required for full activity is called the full scope for a species. The habitability of water can then be measured by the percentage of full scope for the species or $(C_O - C_L)/(C_a - C_L)$, where C_L is the incipient lethal oxygen rate, C_a is the oxygen consumption rate necessary for full activity and C_O is the oxygen consumption rate associated with a particular water quality. High oxygen levels in the water can support the full scope of fish activities, but at some critical level of dissolved oxygen the percentage of full scope for the fish begins to fall rapidly. A half-scope criterion has often been suggested as a standard of water quality (Jones, 1964).

Besides conducting laboratory experiments one can observe the changes that have occurred in the fish populations of various water bodies over time. Such data, however, are often incomplete in specifying the exact quality of the water and come either from commercial fish catches, which do not represent a true sample of the fish population, or from casual observation.

Furthermore, even when the data are good it is difficult to separate the effects of pollution from other causes of species extinction. The sturgeon in the Great Lakes, for example, were wiped out, not by pollution, but by overfishing. These fish, regarded as a nuisance by early fishermen because they fouled their

Figure 9
Hypothetical relationship between the oxygen concentration
in water and the oxygen consumption rate of a fish (from J.R. Jones,
1964, 20)

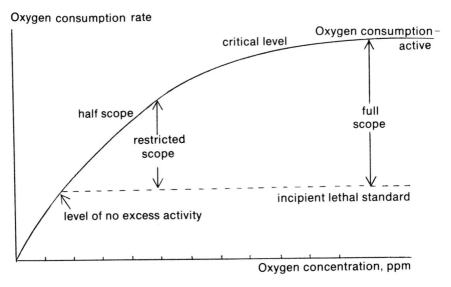

nets, were caught in great numbers and often left to rot on the beach because of their lack of commercial value. Other species have been hurt in the Lakes because of the invasion of the lamprey eel or the use of deep-water trap netting.

The decline of the fish population may be shown, not in terms of total catches, but in the change of the species that are caught. Total annual Ontario production of fish from the Great Lakes has fluctuated around 55 million lbs annually for many years, but the value of the catch has decreased. Even Lake Erie, the most polluted of the Lakes, continues to produce about 35 million lbs per year of fish in Ontario, but the catch now consists of yellow perch, smelt, carp, sheepshead, and white bass instead of the lake herring, blue pike, sauger, whitefish, and walleye caught some twenty years ago.

No reliable existing study relates the commercial value of the fish caught in these lakes with the levels of pollution in them. Such a study would measure the decrease in the sustainable yield of a certain species caused by an increase in pollution and then place a value on it. This value is not the market price of the fish but the net profit to fishermen who catch them, because the men and materials used in catching them could be used productively elsewhere in the economy if the fishing industry were to decline, so that the value they contribute to the price of the fish should not be counted as a loss when the species disappears. Of course this assumes that the necessary relocation would occur relatively quickly and costlessly. If it did not, as it may not in certain areas where fishing is the primary industry, some additional cost would have to be added for this adjustment. Finally, we should subtract from the losses previously calculated the increase in the value of the sustainable yield of species that have increased because of the elimination of their predators and their superior ability to adapt to poor water quality.

One interesting study relates the water quality in Yaquina Bay, Oregon, to the value of the recreational fishery in these waters. Stevens (1966) used the Clawson method to calculate a demand curve for sport fishing in Yaquina Bay. In this method the number of fishing days per ten thousand population for a twelve-month period in 1963-4 was calculated for areas at various distances from the bay. An imputed price was then put on each day equal to the sum of travel costs valued at six cents per mile and actual expenditures at restaurants, lodgings, and marinas. On the assumption that individuals would react in the same way to an increase in these imputed costs as they would to an admission charge for the fishery, Stevens then calculated the number of angling days for each hypothetical admissions charge. This curve is shown as D_0 in Figure 10. Respondents to a questionnaire were then asked the number of days they would have fished at the bay if the average catch had been decreased. If the average catch were reduced by 50 per cent, for instance, the demand curve would have fallen to D_1.

At this point, however, Stevens made a serious error. He calculated the loss from decreased water quality as the amount of the crosshatched triangle in the figure rather than as the whole area between the demand curves. But even those fishing days that would have occurred with the lower quality water are worth less to the fishermen than they would have been with the higher quality water. Thus he erroneously finds that the value of the loss of this part of the recreational fishery is $5,279 per year instead of $28,500 per year.

Recreational benefits

One of the most important benefits of pollution abatement in heavily populated areas with few water bodies suitable for recreation is the increase in the recreational use of the improved water. In a study of the benefits of abatement in the Delaware estuary, for instance, it was found that an increase of three milligrams per litre of dissolved oxygen could be justified on the basis of increased boating alone. The demand for a recreational resource can be measured by several interesting techniques which are easily adapted to account for the benefit of increased quality of the resource.

Throughout this section we assume that the recreational use of these resources produces no externalities in itself: that boating does not foul the

Figure 10
Demand for a recreational fishery, Yaquina Bay, Oregon
(from Stevens, 1966, 179)

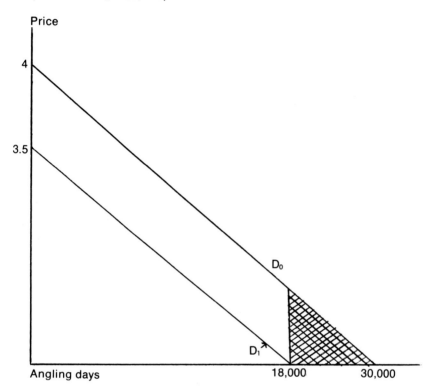

waters nor noise disturb area residents. Furthermore we do not consider the benefit to an individual community of the increased trade that the development of a recreational facility may provide on the ground that this is mainly an income redistribution effect best handled separately from the consideration of the direct benefits derived from the resource. We attempt to determine how the use of a resource varies with the quality of the water and how this increased use can be valued.

The primary methods used to evaluate these resources are based on the construction of willingness-to-pay schedules like those discussed in the first section of this chapter. When an individual decides how often he will swim at a particular beach he considers a number of factors. He is influenced by the cost of travelling there, the value to him of the time spent getting to the swimming area, and the pleasure or displeasure associated with the trip. He considers the admission charge, if any, the quality of the water, and the other facilities present, as well as the characteristics of other beaches in the region. If the cost of another day of swimming outweighs the enjoyment from that day he will not swim any more at this area. If we assume that there are decreasing marginal benefits from additional days of swimming the individual will swim until the value of the benefits of another day of swimming exactly equals the cost to him of this day. For each of the days of swimming previous to this marginal day, however, the individual will have enjoyed some net benefit. If we could discern this net benefit for each day we could charge him an admission fee equal to this amount without influencing his decision. Thus a plot of the maximum admission fee he would pay for each day of swimming would yield a schedule such as DD in Figure 5. This would be his willingness-to-pay schedule for the use of the beach. The total area under this curve DOD represents the value of the beach to the individual.

If the water quality were improved the value of the beach to him would rise, and he would be willing to pay more for each day of swimming. This would be reflected in an increase in his willingness-to-pay schedule to $D'D'$, and the net benefit to him of the improvement in water quality would be the area between the curves $D'D'DD$. This whole area is a measure of his benefits because there is no admission charge, and not only will he swim at the beach more often but each time he does swim will be more enjoyable than before.

Aggregating vertically all the demand curves for potential users of the beach will produce the total value of the added water quality to society. Of course, if increased quality at this beach means decreased attendance at another beach the loss of benefits there must be subtracted from the gain at this facility.

Clawson and Knetsch (1966) have developed a method for estimating the willingness-to-pay function on the basis of the imputed costs of using a facility. They calculate the cost of the trip for various distance zones by calculating a cost per mile for the round trip and food and lodging costs using statistics on the visits per thousand population by distance travelled to the site. If more than one site is visited on a particular trip or more than one activity engaged in the costs of the trip must be allocated among the different sites or uses. They then assume that people will react to a one-dollar increase in the price of admission in the same way that they would react to a one-dollar increase in travel costs. This allows the calculation of a hypothetical attendance figure for each admission charge by applying the frequency-of-use statistics for the further regions to the closer regions. Thus, if there is a population of ten thousand people at a distance such that the travel costs are six dollars and their participation rate is ten swimming days per thousand people and there is another area with a participation rate of nine swimming days per thousand population at a distance such that the travel costs amount to seven dollars, an admission charge of one dollar will mean that instead of swimming to a total of one hundred days per year, the people at the shorter distance will swim only ninety days. Similarly, the people farther away will have the participation rate of those still a dollar farther out.

There are many good applications of this method (ibid.), but only the Yaquina Bay study discussed earlier includes water quality as a variable. A number of problems arise in the use of this method. First, differences in taste among the population zones are frequently neglected, although they may be incorporated by the use of demographic characteristics as well as distances travelled in the regression. The method also assumes that travel costs and admissions fees are regarded in the same way by the consumer, which may not be the case. Furthermore, the time costs of travel are neglected because of a lack of information on their value to different individuals, and this results in a downward bias in the curve. Cesario and Knetsch (1970) suggest that if a particular relationship between time and travel costs can be postulated, this bias could be eliminated, although one would then be open to errors due to misspecification of this relationship. The method also neglects the relatively greater recreational opportunities within the appropriate travel-cost radius available to those located further away from the site, and this too results in a downward bias in the curve.

Another method used to estimate the willingness-to-pay schedule is to question people using the site about their reactions to various admission fees. An excellent example of the use of this method is the study by Davis (Knetsch and Davis, 1966) of the value of the Maine woods. Such a survey, however, requires people to answer hypothetical questions, which they may be ill prepared to do. Furthermore, the sample is biased by interviewing only those already present at the site.

Still another frequently used method is multiple regression analysis, explaining the frequency of participation in a particular activity by such characteristics of the respondent as age, sex, race, income level, the availability of facilities, and the quality of these facilities. The results of such a study can then be used to predict the increase in participation in a certain activity with an increase in the quality of the water. This method, however, gives only the difference in total quantity consumed, $OD' - OD$ in Figure 5; it does not provide any guide to the valuation of these units or to the increased value of the intramarginal units OD.

The study by Davidson, Adams, and Seneca (1966) of the Delaware estuary is of this type. Michigan data were used to estimate the probability that an individual would participate in an activity at least once during the year. The independent variables in the study were age, income, sex, number and ages of children, water area per capita in the region, amount of coastline, and an expert's rating of the quality of the facilities available. These regressions gave very unsatisfactory results for all three activities (swimming, boating, and fishing) with the highest R^2 being 0.280. But a significant relationship was found between the amount of water per capita in the region and the probability that a person would participate in boating and fishing.

The demographic data for the Delaware estuary area were then used with these regressions to predict the change in participation rates that would result from making water quality of the estuary suitable for boating or swimming. It was assumed that a dissolved oxygen level of 3ppm was adequate for boating, 4ppm for fishing, and 5ppm for swimming. The area of the estuary was added to the water-per-acre figure when the water quality reached this level and the increase in participation calculated. When the increased participation rates were multiplied by the population and by the average number of days of activity per participant, the increase in boating or fishing days when the water quality was improved was obtained.

This study is filled with heroic assumptions. The basic regressions used to calculate the participation rates have questionable significance and the use of critical *DO* levels for different activities with no increase in these activities for any higher levels of water quality is hard to justify. Still, this method does hold some advantages. If the data were available to do an adequate study of the participation rates, it could be used in other areas of the country without repeating the whole study, a definite saving in research time and money that might compensate for the difficulty of placing a value on the increased-activity days once they are estimated.

The final method of measuring the recreational benefits of abatement is the property-value method described at length in the air pollution section. Where we are interested in the quality of a body of water with little public access, where the recreational opportunities are enjoyed mainly by surrounding property owners, the value of an improvement in quality should be capitalized into the value of neighbouring properties. Knetsch (1964) studies the creation of a reservoir in an area where the recreational opportunities would be enjoyed mainly by local residents. He compares the value of sites close to existing reservoirs with those distant from them and found that building the dam would have a significant positive effect on property values. A method such as this might well be used to evaluate water quality improvements in specific Ontario cottage country lakes.

THE BENEFIT OF ABATEMENT BY A POLLUTER

The benefits of abatement previously discussed in this section are the benefits of improving the ambient air or water quality in a particular region; but a polluter's abatement is defined as a reduction in emissions. It is important to realize before considering the cost of abatement how the two models are combined to determine the optimal amount of abatement by the firm.

We can put this problem formally by hypothesizing a region which we will divide into n areas of homogeneous air quality and m factories located throughout it. The damage in each area of the city is a function of the ambient air quality in that area: $D_i = D_i(Q_i)$, $i = 1 \dots n$. The total damage in the region is then the sum of the damages to each area. $D = \Sigma_{i=1}^n D_i$. The benefit of abatement or damage avoided can be expressed as $\bar{D} - D$ where $\bar{D}$ is the damage when there is no abatement. The cost of abatement to each firm is a function of the effluent which it emits, $C_j = C_j(E_j)$, $j = 1 \dots m$, and the total cost of abatement to society is the sum of these costs: $C = \Sigma_{i=1}^m C_j$.

The necessary connection between these cost and benefit functions is a dispersion model that relates the effluents discharged by each firm to the air quality in each region: $Q_i = Q_i(E_1, E_2, \dots, E_m)$.

Maximizing the net benefits from abatement requires maximizing $(\bar{D} - D) - C$ with respect to the effluents discharged by each firm:

$$\text{Max} \quad (\bar{D} - D) - C = \bar{D} - \sum_{i=1}^n D_i [Q_i (E_1 \dots E_m)] - \sum_{i=1}^n C_j (E_j).$$

The first-order conditions for a maximum will be

$$\frac{\partial (\bar{D} - D - C)}{\partial E_j} = \sum_{i=1}^n \frac{\partial D_i}{\partial Q_i} \frac{\partial Q_i}{\partial E_j} - \frac{\partial C_j}{\partial E_j} = 0, \quad j = 1, \dots, m.$$

This will yield a system of m equations in the m unknown emissions which can be solved for the optimal discharges of each plant. If the damage function is linear in air quality the jth equation will be a function only of the jth emission level, and each equation can be solved separately by setting the marginal damage done by the firm equal to the marginal cost of abatement. Otherwise the whole system must be solved simultaneously. Once the optimal emissions from each firm and the optimal air quality in any area have been determined, one may choose any of the policies described in the previous chapter to bring this situation about.

SUMMARY AND CONCLUSIONS

This chapter has indicated the need for more research on the benefits of pollution control. The first section of this chapter classifies the benefits of pollution abatement as reducing direct costs and costs of avoidance, pointing out that both effects are often spread through the market to those not directly affected by the pollution. These damages can be measured directly through the use of statistical techniques to relate the expenditure on an item, frequency of performance of a task, or probability of an event occurring to the quality of ambient air or water and other relevant variables. Alternatively, the question-naire method can be used to derive either directly or indirectly the willingness-to-pay or demand schedule for the environment. These schedules would be the same if income effects were small, if both were measured correctly, and if individuals knew and could place a value on all of the effects of pollution. Because pollution abatement is a public good, society's damage or demand func-tion is the sum of the individual functions for every member of society. The only real theoretical problems that remain, then, are those of project design: what measure of pollution should be used in such studies and what other vari-ables should be held constant?

The current state of the literature, however, admits only the broadest type of conclusion. Although much laboratory evidence of the damage to materials by air pollution exists, most carefully constructed studies find no significant effect of air pollution on the frequencies of cleaning and repair of affected items. This could be because our data on ambient air quality is too poor to show such an association or because the effect of air pollution is so small in comparison with other factors that the usual statistical study will not be able to discern it.

Although damage to vegetation and livestock by certain pollutants is well documented, only one study places an economic value on the loss. This study of the loss to citrus growers and cattlemen in Florida (Crocker, 1969) uses a property-value method of estimating the loss in the productive capacity of the land. Such studies are well suited to measuring the long-run damages from pollu-tion since they evaluate not just the direct loss from plant or livestock damage in a given year but also the difference between the present value of future profits from a piece of land in the absence of pollution and in its best alternative use with a given level of pollution.

Health damage is found to be one of the most significant costs of air pollu-tion. Although studies abound relating the level of pollution to mortality and morbidity rates, many deal only with episodic incidents and thus are not appro-priate for measuring long-run damages, and only one (Lave and Seskin, 1970) adequately takes into account all of the relevant variables other than air pollu-tion. Even the best of these studies is used only to estimate the health costs to society of the existing level of pollution. A methodology suggested by Ridker (1967) was given for deriving a benefit schedule from the relationship between pollution and mortality or morbidity rates.

Finally, a method is proposed which would take into account all of the above types of damage. In this method the price differential for residential or other properties is explained by the characteristics of the property including its ambient air quality. The portion of the differential due to air pollution then gives a maximum figure for the present value of the damages from pollution. Here the main difficulty is in determining exactly which damages are being discounted in the value of the house since those that are not should be added to the damage measured in this way to arrive at a total benefit function.

Our knowledge of the benefits of water pollution abatement is as limited as that of the benefits of air quality improvement. All the evidence points to minimal benefits for industrial and domestic use of this resource. The value of the injury to aquatic life may be much more severe but, as in the case of material damage by air pollution, little beyond laboratory evidence is available. Unlike the materials-damage case the problem here is not that well conceived studies have shown no significant results but that there have been no such studies. The type of study which is needed on the value of the loss of commercial fisheries was outlined as an example.

Surprisingly, the best work done on the value of water quality improvement seems to be in the area of its recreational and aesthetic uses. Even the value of reduced aquatic life in recreational fisheries is better known than that in commercial fisheries. Several methods are presented to derive a willingness-to-pay schedule for a given resource, and it is noted that shifts in this schedule when water quality is improved provide a measure of the social benefit of this improvement. The existence of a number of good studies illustrating these methods is encouraging since the recreational and aesthetic benefits of water quality improvement may be most important in areas of high population and limited water resources.

Finally, this chapter points out the important role of the dispersion model in relating the benefit of improved air quality to the benefit of abatement by a particular firm. This model, along with the question whether the benefit function is separable or non-separable, is crucial for the determination of the optimal level of abatement by the firms in an area and the optimal choice of control policy.

The need for further research on benefit estimation is great. First and foremost is the need for adequate data on the levels of air and water pollution in each region taken at frequent intervals. This data must report more than the levels of one or two pollutants since different pollutants may be most important for different problems. Air pollution data, for instance, should include pollutants from automotive emissions as well as the standard sulphur dioxide and particulates. Water quality data should include dissolved oxygen, turbidity, pH, heavy-metal content, temperature, and so on.

Once such data are available we can expect a rapid increase in our knowledge of the nature of the benefit function. The most promising area for immediate work seems to be the extension of the use of the property-value method to the problems of agricultural, recreational and aesthetic damages. The evaluation of the loss of commercial fisheries and the extension of the existing studies on health injuries into value estimates should also be given top priority. Only when such basic research has been carried out will we be in a position to recommend specific policies for existing problems.

4
Costs of pollution control

INTRODUCTION

The cost of pollution abatement is a necessary input to the determination of optimal levels of pollution. In addition, these costs are useful in determining the economic impact of alternate environmental policies. Because the knowledge of abatement costs is important, a review of the existing abatement-cost literature, emphasizing methodology in some cases and empirical results in others, seems relevant.

The bulk of published control-cost studies have been for pollutants and sources that can be associated with a standardized abatement technology. As a result, these studies have tended to deal with a rather small subset of polluters and pollutants. In the field of air pollution control, for example, most control-cost studies deal with the abatement of sulphur oxides or particulates from thermal power plant flue gases. Most published water pollution control-cost studies deal with the abatement of biochemical oxygen demand (BOD) or suspended solids (SS) by wastewater treatment plants. The literature surveyed in this chapter reflects this emphasis.

Individual abatement-cost studies for more exotic pollutants or for the standard pollutants at sources other than thermal power plants or wastewater treatment plants are not generally available in the control-cost literature. Those that are available typically yield single-point cost estimates for a particular type of plant under specialized conditions. Hence, control-cost estimates for many point sources may require either the employment of an engineering-consulting firm or comparison with a similar installation that has already achieved adequate abatement.

The next section of this chapter discusses costs as a function of two explanatory variables: plant capacity and units of pollutant abated. The optimal level of pollution abatement should be determined from the cost per unit of pollution abatement. That section therefore demonstrates how cost schedules stated in terms of plant capacity for various levels of abatement can be used to derive the cost-abatement relationship. It also deals with the theoretical derivation of the abatement-cost schedule, and in doing so shows that all alternative abatement techniques must be taken into account when defining least-cost methods of reducing emissions. Increasing assimilative capacity is incorporated as an abatement alternative. Part of this section examines the economics of high smoke stacks.

The third section defines the cost categories commonly used in the control-cost literature and some of the problems associated with deriving them. It also discusses previous control-cost studies showing the available methodologies and the empirical results established so far. Various other problems that arise in determining the social costs of abatement are also discussed.

COST FUNCTIONS OVERVIEW

Selection of a dependent variable
There is a major distinction between point-cost estimates and cost functions. Point estimates are single-valued costs for a particular pollution control process, assuming a fixed set of design parameters. For example, Slack et al. (1972, 166) suggest a capital cost of $40/KW for the abatement of sulphur dioxide from power plant flue gases by lime-limestone scrubbing. Cost functions on the other hand show a range of potential costs as a function of various parameters, usually the design capacity of abatement equipment and units of pollution abated. The capacity parameters for wastewater plants are millions of gallons treated per day or the population equivalent that can be served. The most common air pollution capacity parameter is designed flue gas flow in actual cubic feet per minute (acfm).

Costs as a function of capacity and units abated are shown in Figure 11. Figure 11a shows annual abatement-cost curves for two plants A and B with waste emissions of the same concentration but different total quantity and with abatement equipment of different design capacities. Plant A generates more waste and has larger-capacity equipment. It also exhibits lower annual costs per unit of capacity at each level of abatement, indicating economies of scale. Points t and s in this figure represent 100 per cent abatement for plants A and B respectively. Design capacity is held constant along curves A and B.

Figure 11b shows annual abatement-cost curves for two plants C and D with waste emissions of the same concentration and abatement equipment that

Figure 11
Total annual control costs: **a**, for two fixed design capacities;
b, for two fixed percentage abatement levels

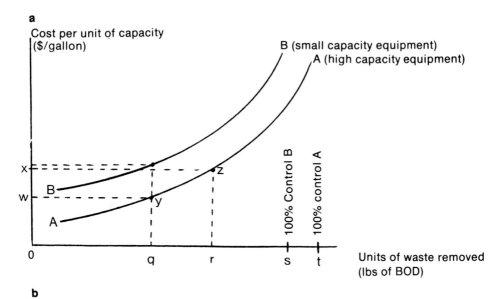

a

Cost per unit of capacity
($/gallon)

B (small capacity equipment)

A (high capacity equipment)

x

w

B

y

A

z

0

q

r

s

t

100% Control B

100% control A

Units of waste removed
(lbs of BOD)

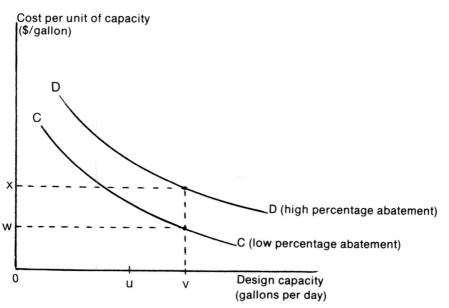

b

Cost per unit of capacity
($/gallon)

D

C

x

w

D (high percentage abatement)

C (low percentage abatement)

0

u

v

Design capacity
(gallons per day)

removes different amounts of the waste. Units of waste removed are constant along curves C and D. Plant D, with higher percentage abatement equipment at each design capacity, exhibits higher annual costs per unit of capacity at each level of designed capacity. These curves show the rise in abatement cost with increasing levels of abatement efficiency.

If one needs the abatement-cost functions to determine the optimal level of pollution abatement rather than the optimal design capacity of this equipment, the relevant independent variable is units of waste removed or removal efficiency, as in Figure 11a. Given a number of functions like C and D it is possible to derive a cost function like A by holding design capacity constant and varying the number of units abated. For a given design capacity such as v in Figure 11b, the cost of a high degree of abatement is x and of a low degree is w. The quantity of waste removed is capacity times pollution concentration times degree of abatement, which are points r and q in Figure 11a. The interaction of cost w with removal q and of cost x with removal r gives points y and z on cost curve A.

Socially optimal levels of pollution should be based on incremental social control costs of reaching various levels of pollution and the corresponding benefits. Such costs are derived from the abatement-cost curves of individual point sources, such as the cost curves presented in Figure 11a. If an ambient environmental quality standard is to be used the individual source abatement cost curve must be aggregated through a dispersion model to produce a total cost curve that can be weighed against the total benefit curve. If individual emission standards are to be enforced the total benefit function must be disaggregated through a dispersion model to produce benefit functions associated with abatement from each source. In either case the source abatement cost curves must be ascertained.

Cost functions with several technical alternatives
A theoretical procedure for deriving a cost-of-abatement function is offered by Kneese and Bower (1968, 93-4, 105-9). This will serve as a frame of reference for the later survey of techniques used in the various empirical studies.

Many alternative methods exist for achieving any given level of environmental quality. These can be classified as increasing the assimilative capacity of the environment (e.g. augmenting stream flow) and reducing the waste load emitted. An environmental authority may consider changing assimilative capacity, but the individual polluter is usually limited to waste treatment, reduced output, introducing process adjustments, and the like. We are concerned with deriving the individual polluter's cost curve, so that augmenting assimilative capacity is ignored in this section.

Assume a waste reduction function of the form

$$Q = f(X_1, X_2 \ldots X_n), \tag{4.1}$$

where Q is the level of waste reduction and X_i $(i = 1, 2 \ldots n)$ represents all methods of abatement. This relationship defines the maximum waste reduction achievable at a given level of operation for each of the control alternatives X_1, $X_2 \ldots X_n$. The profit maximizing firm will try to achieve a given waste reduction Q^* in a manner that minimizes cost:

$$C = P_1 X_1 + P_2 X_2 \ldots + P_n X_n, \tag{4.2}$$

where P_i is the cost per unit of waste reduction by method i $(i = 1, 2, 3 \ldots n)$, X_i is the level of operation of process i, or the quantity of input i used, and C is the total cost of abatement. Hence the firm will minimize the following Lagrangian:

$$Z = P_1 X_1 + P_2 X_2 + \ldots P_n X_n + \lambda [Q^* - f(X_1, X_2 \ldots X_n)]. \tag{4.3}$$

This expression is minimized by equating all the partial derivatives to zero. Assuming only two alternative abatement techniques and defining them as units of production forgone X_1 and increasing size of treatment facilities X_2, the following first-order conditions result:

$$P_1 - \lambda \frac{\partial f}{\partial X_1} = 0,$$

$$P_2 - \lambda \frac{\partial f}{\partial X_2} = 0,$$

$$Q^* - f(X_1, X_2) = 0. \tag{4.4}$$

These three simultaneous equations can be solved for X_1, X_2, and λ.

The optimizing rule derived from the first two equations in (4.4) is

$$P_1 \Big/ (\partial f / \partial X_1) = P_2 \Big/ (\partial f / \partial X_2), \tag{4.5}$$

which means that the incremental cost of abatement by the two processes must be equal.[1] This is the firm's rule for minimizing abatement costs.

1 An environmental authority must equate the marginal costs of all alternatives facing the firm with each other and with that of augmenting assimilative capacity.

Graphically, equation (4.1) can be shown by a series of isoquants, like KK' and CC' shown in Figure 12a. Each isoquant represents a constant waste reduction along its length. Equation (4.2) is represented by lines like AA' and BB' which represent a constant level of costs along their length.[2] These isocost lines indicate the combinations of X_1 and X_2 that can be purchased at a given cost.

Points Y and Y' represent combinations of X_1 and X_2 that will achieve different levels of abatement at least cost. The mapping of such optimal points as Q varies is called the expansion path for pollution control and is shown by the dotted line in Figure 12a. This expansion path is defined by equation (4.5).

The firm's abatement-cost function can be derived by simultaneously solving equations (4.1) and (4.5) and determining the optimal levels of inputs X_1^* and X_2^* as functions of P_1, P_2, and Q. Substituting these equations into equation (4.2) gives costs as a function of unit input costs and output. Since unit input costs are assumed known and constant this is an abatement-cost function dependent on the quantity of waste reduction:

$$C = g(Q). \tag{4.6}$$

This is equivalent to transforming the expansion path of Figure 12a, i.e. YY', into cost-abatement space, as demonstrated in Figure 12b. The key point of this analysis is that many alternative techniques may enable the firm to achieve any desired level of abatement. It may add control devices, vary the productive process, or change inputs. All of these alternatives must be included in the firm's 'true' abatement-cost curve.

Increasing environmental assimilative capacity

Environmental assimilative capacity can be increased in many ways. The prominent water pollution techniques are to augment stream flow and to reaerate rivers and lakes. The corresponding technique for air pollution is high stacks that reduce peak pollution concentrations but spread the pollution over a wider area. The individual polluter who faces an effluent charge or standard based on total waste discharge alone will not consider these alternatives because they will not be included in his cost curves. It is clear, however, that from society's point of view if these techniques reduce pollution damage they should be considered. This section describes how, with the aid of the individual firm cost curves described in the next section and a dispersion model, these alternatives can be

2 For simplicity the isocost curves are drawn as straight lines because of the assumption of a fixed per-unit cost P_i. This assumption is not essential to the analysis.

Figure 12
Derivation of the total-cost-of-abatement curve

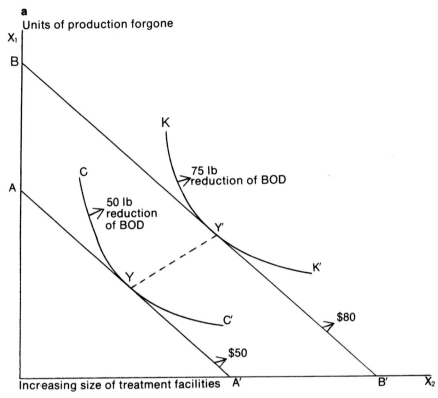

a

Units of production forgone

X_1

Increasing size of treatment facilities

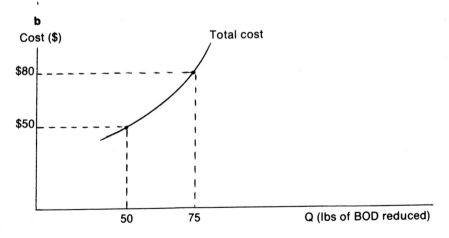

b

Cost ($)   Total cost

included in the socially optimal choice of abatement techniques and emission levels.[3]

Consider an environmental authority that desires to minimize the social costs of pollution at a single point Z downstream from a polluting firm. The goal is to maximize

$$\text{NB} = B - C,\qquad(4.7)$$

where NB is net social benefit, B is the social benefit of water quality at point Z, and C is the total cost of control. The authority currently imposes an effluent charge on the polluting firm that equates the marginal cost of abatement and the marginal benefit of abatement. It is assumed that the authority is aware of the possibility of augmenting stream flow f, and it tries to use this technique in an optimal manner.

The following relationships are assumed to be known by the authority:

$$B = B(Q),$$
$$Q = Q(e,f),$$
$$C = C_1(e) + C_f(f),\qquad(4.8)$$

where Q is ambient water quality and is a function of the firm's emissions e, and the river flow f. C_1 is the total cost of abating[4] to emission rate e, and C_f is the total cost of augmenting stream flow to f.

This system is optimized by maximizing

$$\text{NB} = B[Q(e,f)] - C_1(e) - C_f(f).\qquad(4.7')$$

The following first-order conditions result:

$$\frac{dB}{dQ}\frac{\partial Q}{\partial e} = \frac{dC_1}{de},$$

$$\frac{dB}{dQ}\frac{\partial Q}{\partial f} = \frac{dC_f}{df}.\qquad(4.9)$$

---

3 Although the discussion will be in terms of augmenting stream flow it could be carried out in a similar manner for other methods of increasing assimilative capacity. The effect of augmentation is to reduce the concentration of pollution for a given amount of emissions.

4 These are the control costs that were derived above.

These indicate, respectively, that the marginal benefit of reducing effluent e must equal the marginal cost of reducing effluent and that the marginal benefit of increasing stream flow must equal the marginal cost of increasing stream flow. Conditions (4.9) must be fulfilled simultaneously in order to maximize (4.7$'$).

These optimizing rules can also be stated as

$$\frac{dB}{dQ} = \frac{dC_1}{de} \bigg/ \frac{\partial Q}{\partial e} = \frac{dC_f}{df} \bigg/ \frac{\partial Q}{\partial f}. \tag{4.10}$$

Intuitively, condition (4.10) implies that assimilative capacity should be expanded until incremental cost of improving water quality in this way equals the cost of doing so by reducing emissions at the polluting firm.[5] These must also simultaneously equal the incremental benefits of changing water quality.

The optimal level of pollution emissions by the firm and the optimal effluent charge EC occurs where the marginal cost of waste reduction equals the marginal benefit of waste reduction at that firm:

$$\frac{dB}{dQ} \frac{\partial Q}{\partial e} = \frac{dC_1}{de} = EC_1. \tag{4.11}$$

This condition can be derived by maximizing (4.7$'$) subject to a given level of stream flow, say f_0. Augmentation of stream flow will affect the relationship between stream quality and emissions from the firm. The result of increasing augmentation is to reduce $\partial Q/\partial e$ and hence to reduce the marginal benefits of abatement, the optimal level of waste reduction at the firm, and abatement costs C_1. If multiple points of pollution emissions exist along the river such cost reductions will take place at each such point. Of course, these cost savings will only occur if the authority adjusts the effluent charge downward in an optimal manner for each of these point sources as augmentation is increased.

---

5 Kneese and Bower (1968, 192), discussing the optimal augmentation of stream flow, state that 'the agency, if acting efficiently, would increase assimilative capacity in such a way that the marginal cost of the last increment in capacity to control the effect of a waste would be equal to the effluent charge on that waste, which in turn is equal to the marginal cost of waste control at outfalls.' This implies an optimal condition of

$$\frac{dC_f}{df} = EC_1 = \frac{dC_1}{de} = \frac{dB}{dQ} \frac{\partial Q}{\partial e}.$$

This, however, is only in agreement with condition (4.10), the 'true' condition for optimality, if $\partial Q/\partial e = \partial Q/\partial F$. It seems likely that this condition would not hold and therefore that the Kneese and Bower condition is not sufficient for efficiency.

Increasing assimilative capacity by augmenting stream flow, is not often considered as a method of abatement by individual point sources because it involves a public goods problem. If firm j chose to augment stream flow it would pay all the associated costs but reap only a small portion of the gains. Other polluters downstream from j would benefit from j's action, since the optimal emissions for each affected point source will now be greater. Since all the benefits of j's augmentation cannot be appropriated by j, he will not do it even when it is socially desirable. Hence the socially optimal use of this alternative requires government intervention.

Another technique often associated with increased assimilative capacity is the construction of high smoke stacks. This technique, however, does not incur the public goods problem. Nevertheless, this alternative will only be considered in cases where the environmental protection agency adjusts effluent charges or standards to reflect lower damages from greater dispersion, or where ambient air quality standards are the basis of regulation. Because one firm's use of high stacks does not alter the pollution damage caused by any other polluter (except where damages are a non-linear function of concentration), all the benefits of this action can be appropriated by the party incurring the costs.

If, as is more probable in the real world, the pollution policy deals with stack emissions rather than ambient concentrations, high stacks will not benefit the polluter. Under these circumstances individual emitters are not likely to build stacks of optimal height or to consider this as an abatement alternative. Hence the socially optimal use of this alternative requires careful drafting of regulations.

There is some question whether increasing stack height always increases assimilative capacity and hence reduces damages. Proponents of this alternative claim that the effluent from high stacks will be dispersed and rendered harmless at high levels. Opponents believe that the emissions will not be rendered harmless by dispersion and that the effect of the stack is to spread damages over a wider area.

Increasing the height of a smoke stack at a point source will have two effects: air quality improves in the zone initially damaged by emissions, i.e. the inner fume zone, because the pollution disperses more before reaching the ground; pollution concentrations increase in areas previously unaffected or only marginally affected by emissions from this source. The choice of optimal stack height must consider both of these effects.

The following relationships are assumed to be known by the environmental authority:

$$B_I = B_I(Q_I),$$

$$B_0 = B_0(Q_0),$$
$$Q_I = Q_I(e, h),$$
$$Q_0 = Q_0(e, h),$$
$$C = C(e, h), \tag{4.12}$$

where B_I is the benefit of air quality Q_I in the inner fume zone, B_0 is the social benefit of air quality Q_0 in areas outside the inner fume zone [6], C is the cost of control, e is emissions from the firm, and h is the height of the stack.

Optimizing this system requires the authority to maximize pollution benefits in both regions minus the costs of control at the polluting source. The authority can ensure a smoke stack of optimal height by adjusting an effluent charge in an optimal manner. This optimization requires maximizing net benefits:

$$\text{NB} = B_I[Q_I(e, h)] + B_0[Q_0(e, h)] - C(e, h). \tag{4.13}$$

The following first-order conditions result:

$$\frac{dB_I}{dQ_I} \frac{\partial Q_I}{\partial e} + \frac{dB_0}{dQ_0} \frac{\partial Q_0}{\partial e} = \frac{\partial C}{\partial e}, \tag{4.14}$$

$$\frac{dB_I}{dQ_I} \frac{\partial Q_I}{\partial h} + \frac{dB_0}{dQ_0} \frac{\partial Q_0}{\partial h} = \frac{\partial C}{\partial h}. \tag{4.15}$$

These indicate, respectively, that to maximize net benefits (4.13), the combined marginal benefits in both regions of a decline in emissions for any given stack height and the combined marginal benefits in both regions of increasing stack height must equal the marginal cost of doing so.

Condition (4.14) yields an optimal effluent charge by the authority. For the most efficient solution, condition (4.15) must also be simultaneously fulfilled. In general,

$$\frac{\partial Q_I}{\partial h} > 0, \quad \frac{\partial Q_0}{\partial h} < 0, \quad \frac{\partial Q_I}{\partial e} < 0, \quad \text{and} \frac{\partial Q_0}{\partial e} < 0.$$

6 The inner fume zone is defined as the region in which $\partial Q_1/\partial h > 0$. The areas previously unaffected, i.e. prior to increasing stack height, are defined such that $\partial Q_0/\partial h < 0$. This boundary, where the derivative of concentration with respect to stack height is zero, will move out as stack height increases. In the text, however, we assume that the boundary between these areas is fixed, so that the analysis is valid for small increments in stack height about the specified height.

Furthermore, the magnitudes of $\partial Q_I/\partial e$ and $\partial Q_0/\partial e$ are affected by h. As the height of the stack is increased $\partial Q_I/\partial e$ increases and benefits increase. Meanwhile, $\partial Q_0/\partial e$ decreases and benefits decline. Thus,

$$\frac{dB_0}{dQ_0}\frac{\partial Q_0}{\partial h}$$

is a cost, and the optimality conditions can be rewritten as

$$\frac{dB_I}{dQ_I} = \left(\frac{\partial C}{\partial e} - \frac{dB_0}{dQ_0}\frac{\partial Q_0}{\partial e}\right)\bigg/ \frac{\partial Q_I}{\partial e} = \left(\frac{\partial C}{\partial h} - \frac{dB_0}{dQ_0}\frac{\partial Q_0}{\partial h}\right)\bigg/ \frac{\partial Q_I}{\partial h}. \qquad (4.16)$$

Condition (4.16) implies that stack height should be increased until the incremental cost of improving air quality in the inner fume zone in this way, including damages in the outer zone, equals the incremental cost, including benefits in the outer zone, of increasing air quality in the inner fume zone by reducing emissions at the polluting firm. These must also simultaneously equal the incremental benefits of changing air quality in the inner fume zone. These conditions for optimality point out the necessity of taking into account the damages caused in regions distant from the polluting firm by higher stacks.

EMPIRICAL COST STUDIES

Control-cost categories
Most empirical studies of abatement cost are organized on the basis of accounting cost items. The cost categories usually identified are capital investment, operation and maintenance, capital charges, and depreciation. The first three of these are itemized in Table 9.

The chief data sources for most of these items, and in particular for capital investment items, are engineering journals, manufacturers of equipment, consulting firms, and users of control equipment (Edminsten and Bunyard, 1970, 446).

1 / Capital investment costs
Capital investment includes all relevant expenditures from the beginning of planning until the equipment or process starts actual operation. Costs typically included in this category are outlined in Table 9. Most of these items are self-explanatory, but a few need further elaboration.

'Engineering' means all engineering expenditures from field studies to supervision of the project. 'Interest during construction' allows for borrowing in advance of the completion of the project. 'Contingencies' vary depending on the stage of project completion when the cost study is done. Cost studies based on prototypes and pilot plants characteristically allow for larger contingencies (Kuiper, 1971, 62).

TABLE 9

Accounting items for pollution control

Capital investment	Operation and maintenance	Capital charges
Engineering	Utilities	Taxes
Land	Labour	Insurance
Site preparation	Supplies and materials	Interest
Control hardware	Treatment and disposal	
Interest during construction		
Operating supply inventory		
Auxilary equipment		
Installation		
Structural modification		
Startup		
Contingencies		

The installed capital costs of specific abatement processes vary widely among installations depending on, among other things, the variation in engineering design, transportation costs, plant age, available space, required instrumentation, characteristics of waste stream, and handling of waste materials. Edminsten and Bunyard (1970, 449) imply that purchase costs should be inflated by 135 to 600 per cent to derive total installed capital costs.

Capital investment costs should include all expenditures that would not have occurred but for installing the pollution controls. If installation of the device or process lowers the efficiency of the production process, this should be included either in capital or in operating costs. Few studies have considered this possibility (Dewees 1974, US 1969b).

2 / Operating and maintenance costs

Operating and maintenance costs vary with the degree of utilization of the capital equipment and the user's understanding of and attitudes toward the equipment (Edminsten and Bunyard, 1970, 449). Annual operating costs vary with the designed capacity of the equipment, the suitability and type of abatement equipment, the time that the equipment is in operation, and the cost of utilities. Maintenance costs are required to sustain the equipment at its designed efficiency over its entire life. The wide variance of observed operation and maintenance costs for similar types of abatement equipment (O'Connor and Citarella, 1970) can be attributed to differences in management attitudes toward and understanding of the equipment. Poor accounting procedures for these costs also lead to an arbitrary assignment of costs to pollution control.

Operation and maintenance costs are stated in annual terms. To make capital costs, which are an amount to install some capital equipment that will last for years, commensurable with operating and maintenance costs,[7] capital costs must be annualized.

3 / Annual capital costs

Annual capital costs are fixed costs, comprised of depreciation and capital charges, that must be paid whether the installed equipment is actually operating or not.[8] Capital charges include interest, taxes, and insurance.

Taxes and insurance are easy to compute, but the interest and depreciation variables are controversial because it is not obvious how they should be calculated. The problems are determining a proper interest rate and properly defining depreciation.

Relevant interest rate. The interest rate used in capital cost calculations indicates the opportunity cost of the money required for an investment. In a perfect capital market with no capital rationing each firm would invest until its marginal net return equalled the market rate of interest. Since an alternative course of action is to lend money and earn the market rate of interest, no firm would adopt a project with a yield below the existing interest rate. Even in a perfect market, however, the borrowing and lending rates may diverge because of transaction costs. Then the appropriate interest rate for the determination of annualized control costs is the lending rate, if the firm is a lender, or the borrowing rate, if the firm is a borrower (Hirschleifer, 1970, 197).

Inflation also complicates selection of a rate of interest for determining capital charges. If the market interest rate is 11 per cent but the actual and expected rate of inflation is 6 per cent, the real rate of interest[9] would be 5 per cent. The analysis may be conducted with the real rate of interest and constant

---

7 It is difficult to compare the costs of two projects with different life expectancies except in terms of annual costs. Even if the two processes were expected to be equally durable and they fulfilled the same function, total installed capital costs would not be the correct figures to use for comparison. For example, although the capital cost of a hydro plant is three times as high as that of a steam plant, its annual costs are lower. This phenomenon is explained by lower annual depreciation, insurance, and maintenance and operating costs (Kuiper, 1971, 61).

8 It seems likely that the physical component of depreciation varies with equipment utilization and thus should be included in the operation and maintenance cost category. The difficulty of separating physical and economic depreciation, however, makes such an approach impracticable.

9 This is the rate of interest that would prevail if everyone expected a zero rate of inflation. The real rate of interest is determined by the growth of productivity and the time preference of society.

base year prices or the nominal rate of interest and prices that inflate by 6 per cent per annum. For practical purposes these two procedures give the same result (Kuiper 1971, 214-16), but discounting with the real rate of interest and assuming constant base year prices is easier.

Depreciation. Straight-line depreciation is used in most pollution control cost studies (Edminsten and Bunyard 1970; US, 1969a). This procedure involves implicitly depositing constant amounts in a sinking fund over the life of the equipment. At the end of this period the value of the fund equals the initial value of the machine. This is a means of amortizing debt, but it has been used as a proxy for annual depreciation of the equipment. Straight-line depreciation, however, fails to reduce annual interest costs as the equipment depreciates over its life. For example, equipment with a life of ten years would be depreciated at 10 per cent per annum. When this is combined with an assumed interest rate of 6 per cent per annum, the total annual capital costs (excluding taxes and insurance) is taken to be 16 per cent of the initial capital costs. But as the machine depreciates over time one would expect the opportunity cost of owning it or the interest costs to decline. Thus this method overestimates annual capital costs by failing to deduct depreciation of equipment from the interest payments over the life of the capital.

An alternative and more accurate procedure is the annuity bond method (Dewees, 1974). This method of determining combined interest and depreciation charges assumes equal annual payments that when discounted over the life of the equipment at the relevant interest rate will yield the pre-tax capital investment. These annual charges are derived with the aid of the following formula:

$$D = \frac{A}{1+r} + \frac{A}{(1+r)^2} + \frac{A}{(1+r)^3} \dots + \frac{A}{(1+r)^n} , \qquad (4.17)$$

where D is total capital investment, A is the combined interest and depreciation cost, r is the real rate of interest, and n is the predetermined life of the control equipment.

Solving equation (4.11) for A yields

$$A = D \frac{r(1+r)^n}{(1+r)^n - 1}. \qquad (4.18)$$

If we use this method and assume that $n = 100$ and $r = 0.06$, the annual capital cost (excluding taxes and insurance) is 13.6 per cent instead of the 16 per cent generated by the straight-line method.

Results of control-cost studies
Control-cost studies can be divided into three methodological groups. Engineering cost studies catalogue necessary equipment and related costs for a particular technology. Often these studies are characterized by single-point cost estimates. Statistical cost studies use regression techniques and generally do not delve into the technical aspects of abatement systems. Finally, systems-approach cost curves attempt to combine all feasible technological abatement alternatives in a programming framework to determine least cost methods.

1 / Engineering studies
Engineering cost studies typically focus on the capital costs of tail-end control methods. In general, these studies also consider operating and maintenance costs, but only superficially, in part because of the scarcity of good accounting data in this area. On the other hand, data on capital costs of various types of tail-end control equipment are readily available from manufacturers and equipment users. Even annual capital costs seem arbitrary in the majority of these studies, with little justification for the choice of interest and depreciation rates. The engineering approach studies, which provide the bulk of the abatement-cost literature, may be subdivided according to whether they are used to derive single-point cost estimates, probabilistic point cost estimates, or trend-line cost estimates.

Single-point cost estimates: A typical engineering cost study is the report on sulphur oxide removal prepared for the US National Air Pollution Control Administration (NAPCA) (US, 1969b). This report presents the cost of lime or limestone wet scrubbing of power plant flue gas, ignoring all other possible techniques. Its authors designed a hypothetical scrubber for various sized plants (200 MW and 1000 MW), assuming a set of base conditions such as the sulphur content of fuel burned, limestone costs, and the temperature to which the flue gas was reheated. The capital requirements for such plants were enumerated and all costs summed to determine total capital requirements. The capital cost for a 200 MW unit in an existing power plant, burning 3.5 per cent sulphur coal, reheating the flue gas to $250°$F, and able to remove 99.5 per cent of the dust and 95 per cent of the sulphur dioxide, was determined to be $13.05/KW (ibid., 8). For a 1000 MW unit in a new plant the capital cost was estimated at $6.32/KW.

Operating costs included raw materials, labour, maintenance, and overhead costs. Annual capital costs included credits for eliminating existing electrostatic precipitators, corrosion, reduction, and charges for thermal losses when limestone is injected into the broiler. The total annual costs for a 200 MW unit in an existing plant were estimated to be $1.31/ton of coal or 0.49 mills/ KWH (ibid., 9).

The rate used to determine annual capital costs was 13⅓ per cent and included depreciation, insurance, taxes, and cost of capital. The cost of capital was defined as the annual percentage of investment the company should receive to maintain its credit, pay a normal return to owners, and ensure the attraction of money for future needs.

Another study (Slack, et al., 1972) has, since the NAPCA study, noted that the cost of limestone scrubbing is difficult to estimate because of rapidly rising construction costs. Pilot plant and engineering studies have subsequently shown the process to be more complicated and difficult than originally considered. The estimated total capital cost for a 200 MW unit in an existing plant rose from the $13.05/KW in the NAPCA study to about $40/KW for a new plant. Total annual cost estimates have risen to $2-$4/ton of coal burned (0.75-1.5 mills/KWH).

Another study of limestone scrubbing followed a methodology similar to that of NAPCA to derive capital costs of $0.5-0.61/KW (Dennis and Bernstein, 1968). This figure was for an 800 MW plant and should be compared with NAPCA's $8.21/KW for a 1000 MW unit in an existing plant. This remarkable divergence between capital-cost estimates for identical technology and similar plant size reflected equally remarkable differences in costs of the various components of the system. Current studies tend to rely more heavily on the cost data suggested in the NAPCA study.

The M.W. Kellogg Co. (1972) estimated capital cost for the four most commercially feasible tail-end control techniques for removing sulphur oxide from flue gas. In addition to limestone scrubbing, these included magnesia base, citrate, and ammonia scrubbing. A 1000 MW plant burning 3.5 per cent sulphur coal was assumed. The costs for the four scrubbing systems were then subdivided into scrubber, scrubber circuit, reheat circuit, fans and ductwork, and valves and expansion joints.

The costs under each of these five headings included major equipment costs; foundations, concrete, steel, buildings, paint, and installation; other costs (construction force, home office, engineering, procurement, insurance, startup, and contractor's fee); and net investment cost.[10]

All the above studies use component accounting to estimate a point cost of an abatement technique for a unit of a particular size used under specified base conditions.

Single-point probabilistic cost estimates. An improvement on this point-cost estimate technique was incorporated in a study comparing costs of limestone scrubbing and catalytic oxidation for removal of sulphur oxide from stack gas (Ezzati, 1974). A scrubbing process must be chosen for a power plant using

10 Net investment is the sum of all the previous costs minus a standard plant deduction.

uncertain cost data for these abatement methods. Since these sulphur oxide abatement processes are currently only in the pilot plant stage, subjective estimates are often made of some cost components, introducing uncertainty into the process cost estimates. One solution is to generate (subjectively) a probability distribution for each cost component. The analyst can then show the maximum, minimum, and most likely cost for each component.

Ezzati used data published by manufacturers of equipment, estimates for similar commercial operations, and data from prototype plants to identify the probability distributions for each cost component. A standard mathematical probability distribution was selected to represent the major cost and revenue elements, based on information from the above sources plus calculations made by the author.

Cost and revenue models were then constructed for both abatement processes. The models were simulated over one thousand times using Monte Carlo methods for the probabilistic components, and the final results (i.e. total annual costs) were presented as probability distributions. The simulations indicated that total annual costs in an 800 MW power plant for the catalytic-oxidation system are $3.14/ton of coal with 95 per cent confidence of falling between $3.01 and $3.27, against $1.72/ton of coal for the limestone scrubbing process with 95 per cent confidence of being between $1.66 and $1.77/ton of coal.

The weakness of Ezzati's methodology is the subjective derivation of the probability distributions for the cost components. Ezzati himself admits the subjective nature of this derivation: 'The solution ... is to generate a probability distribution for each cost element with some confidence expressed as the likelihood that the 'true' cost value will fall somewhere within the range. It is immediately apparent that each estimate is not equally likely to occur, so the analyst weighs each estimate according to his own judgement' (ibid., 66-7).

Another study attempted to determine a range of possible costs for installation of specific equipment (US, 1969a). This report used basic equipment cost data for various methods of controlling particulate air pollutants collected from manufacturers, installers, and operators of the equipment. Cost factors and guidelines were presented, so that after defining the type of collection equipment, its size and efficiency, and various characteristics of the flue gas stream and pollutants, one could determine the total installed cost of control hardware.[11] These guidelines for estimating control hardware costs include only those accounting items most directly associated with control costs and those items definable for general application to all industries. Costs such as engineering and land site preparation were excluded. The purchase costs estimated by this procedure vary by ±20 per cent.

---

11 The guidelines for estimating capital costs and the formulas for operating and maintenance costs are presented in similar form in Edminsten and Bunyard (1970).

Installation costs were 35 to 500 per cent of control hardware purchase cost depending on space availability in existing installations and transportation costs. Annual capital costs were capital costs annualized at 13⅓ per cent.

Maintenance costs are highly variable since they depend on management behaviour. Operating costs varied with (a) gas volume cleaned, (b) pressure drop across the system, (c) the time the device was operated, (d) consumption and cost of electricity, and (e) mechanical efficiency of pumps and fans. The generalized annual operation and maintenance cost equation for an electrostatic precipitator is

$$G = S[JHK + M],$$

where G is annual operating and maintenance costs in dollars, S is design capacity in acfm, J is KW of electricity/acfm, H is annual hours of operation, K is the cost of electricity in dollars per kilowatt hour, and M is the maintenance cost in dollars per acfm. Maintenance costs are presented for each type of equipment, for low, typical, and high efficiencies.

The method suggested in the report for estimating the annual costs of control for a specific source can be outlined as follows (6.30-6.33):

1 Describe the source, including process, fuel, and hours operated.

2 Select the control equipment.

3 Determine the gas flow in acfm at the point of collector location.

4 Estimate the purchase cost for the selected device at required gas volume and control efficiency.

5 Multiply this cost by low, typical, and high installation cost factors and add the results to the estimated total purchase cost to obtain low (C_l), typical (C_t) and high (C_h) total installed costs.

6 Total annual capital costs are depreciation plus capital charges. Annual capital charges (i.e. interest plus insurance and taxes) are 6⅔ per cent. Thus total annual capital cost is obtained by multiplying depreciation and capital charges (0.133) times total installed capital cost.

7 Compute low (G_l), typical (G_t) and high (G_h) operating and maintenance costs from the appropriate formulas.

8 Add typical annual capital cost $(AC_t = 0.133 \times C_t)$ to typical operating and maintenance costs (G_t) to yield the estimated total annual cost of control.

9 A variance of costs about this point estimate is calculated and applied to the total estimated annual cost. The low cost variance (V_l) and high cost variance (V_h) can be computed as follows:

$$V_l = \sqrt{[(AC_t - AC_l)^2 + (G_t - G_l)^2]},$$

$$V_h = \sqrt{[(AC_h - AC_t)^2 + (G_h - G_t)^2]}.$$

These[12] permit the computation of the most probable rather than the extreme range of costs.

10 The high cost variance (V_h) is added to the total estimated annual cost to yield the high cost limit.

11 The low cost variance (V_l) is subtracted from this total estimated cost to yield the low cost estimate.

Basically, these are only estimates of ranges of probable costs for specific types of equipment with design parameters specified. There is no attempt in either study to determine costs as a function of degree of abatement or control efficiency for a particular process or industry.

Trend-line cost estimates. One study of auto pollution (Dewees, 1974) attempted to construct a cost curve by designing and comparing annual costs of nine alternative abatement processes. The annual cost per mile of each process was plotted on a graph against the degree of abatement. A trend line was drawn joining the feasible points to show the exponentially increasing trend of annual costs as abatement efficiency increased.

Another study (Brandt and Mann, 1973) used the trend line to estimate a liquid waste treatment cost function as well as particulate and sulphur oxide abatement-cost functions from data in previously published sources. Brandt and Mann argued that liquid waste treatment cost estimates accurate enough for preliminary evaluation can be made with regard only to the volume of the waste stream ignoring its composition. Engineering point cost estimates reported in the literature were gathered. The capital costs, so determined, were then plotted against system capacity. Two distinct groupings of data resulted. The data for waste flows above 100,000 gallons per day are primarily systems treating aqueous wastes, while below this level they treat non-aqueous wastes. Since treatment methods differ there were, in effect, two separate cost functions. Curves were drawn through the two separate data sets and estimated, although curve-fitting techniques were not used. The resulting capital cost equations were

$$Y = 4800 \ X^{0.63}, \qquad \text{(non-aqueous waste removal)}$$

$$Y = 36 \ X^{0.74}, \qquad \text{(aqueous waste removal)}$$

12 These formulas are taken from the usual definition of the standard error of a linear combination of statistically independent variables.

where Y is capital costs in 1972 dollars and X is the liquid flow rate in gallons per day.[13]

Total annual cost functions were assumed to be 20 per cent of total capital costs, i.e. total annual costs are 20 per cent of total capital cost.

Cost functions for particulate and sulphur oxide pollution control were generated in a similar manner. General categories of control equipment were cited and the costs of each determined from literature sources.

Sulphur oxide abatement data were collected for five processes covering a range of 720,000 standard cubic feet per minute (scfm) to 1,800,000 scfm.[14] The data generally represented sulphur dioxide abatement efficiencies of 90 per cent. The capital cost equations plotted were

$$Y = 200 \ X^{0.85}, \qquad \text{(upper bound)}$$

$$Y = 50 \ X^{0.85}, \qquad \text{(lower bound)}$$

where Y is the capital cost in 1972 dollars and X is the flue gas flow in scfm. The capital cost functions presented for particulate emissions were

$$Y = 25 \ X^{0.85}, \qquad \text{(upper bound)}$$

$$Y = 6 \ X^{0.85}. \qquad \text{(lower bound)}$$

Total annual costs were again calculated as 20 per cent of total capital costs.

The recommended procedure for estimating the annual abatement costs of sulphur oxide (particulates) was (1) to determine the total volume of the waste gas stream containing sulphur oxides (particulates) and adjust to standard conditions (1 atmosphere, $60°F$): (2) to estimate capital costs from the upper bound equation; and (3) to multiply the figure in (2) by 0.20 to determine total annual costs.

The most serious shortcoming of this approach was its failure to consider many important variables, particularly the degree of control. On the positive side, however, this technique may present a reasonable 'ballpark' figure for preliminary estimations.

The problem with the majority of engineering cost studies is that they are single-technology oriented.[15] Many techniques are available to abate most waste

13 Also presented were equations of the same form adjusted upward and downward by 50 per cent. The majority of data points fell within this range.
14 This range is observed in power plant sizes of 400 to 1000 MW.
15 The criticisms levied here against engineering cost studies in general applies to a lesser degree to the last two studies summarized (Dewees, 1974; Brandt and Mann, 1973).

emissions. In addition to tail-end alternatives, these include changing the production process and varying the use of inputs. As was pointed out in the previous section, an emitter's cost function should include all these alternatives. Hence engineering cost studies relate to a firm's cost function only if the abatement technology considered is the dominant method available to the emitter.

2 / Statistical cost studies

These studies statistically analyse the cost-capacity or cost-abatement relationship from the accounting data of operating systems. To the extent that the polluter considers all technical abatement possibilities, these will be included in the derived cost function, remedying the basic defect of the engineering study.

The problems with the statistical approach can best be exemplified by considering the type of data required to attain ideal results (Johnston 1960, 26-7). 1/The time period of each pair of observations should be one in which the output[16] was uniform within the period. 2/Observations on costs and output should be paired so that the cost figure is directly associated with the output figure. 3/A wide spread of output figures is desirable so that cost behaviour could be observed at widely differing output levels. 4/The data output should not be influenced by factors extraneous to the cost-output relationship.[17] For example, the capacity of the treatment facility should be held constant for abatement-cost functions. In deriving the cost-capacity relationship one should hold abatement efficiency constant.[18]

The desired range of output observations suggested by criterion 3 can probably only be obtained from cross-sectional data for a reasonably large number of firms at a given time. The most general criticism that can be levied against the use of cross-sectional data to determine the long-run cost function is that firms of different sizes at any period of time may vary in ways not controlled for in the equations. This variation may result from differences in the age of equipment, the ability of management, including their experience with this equipment, and capacity utilization. To the extent that these factors cannot be included in the model, this method fails to take into account that different firms may be at different stages in their capacity utilization and efficiency levels. Therefore two firms might use apparently identical abatement techniques and yet have different per-unit costs of treatment.

Various attempts to derive statistical cost functions have tried to adjust observed data to correct for these problems. For example, O'Connor and

16 'Output' refers here to either abatement or flow of wastewater treated (capacity).
17 Such extraneous influences are variations in underlying factor prices or technological change.
18 If a particular process is only designed at one level of efficiency, we would want cost-capacity data for that process only.

Citarella (1970) used data from a questionnaire survey of a segment of the steam electric power industry, to estimate the relationship between total installed cost of equipment designed to control fly-ash emissions and installed generating capacity. The data showed that installed costs per kilowatt were significantly higher for units from 1958-62 than from 1963-7. This had resulted from changing technology over this period toward the use of electrostatic precipitators. Hence the analysis of the reported installed cost was limited to twenty electrostatic precipitators installed during period 1963-7.

The most significant variables were those related to size, represented by installed generating capacity. The resulting equation was

$$Y = 7.54 + 2.02X,$$

where Y is the installed cost of the precipitator in thousands of 1967 dollars and X is the associated installed generating capacity in megawatts. The considerable variation in operation and maintenance costs defied a systematic relationship for these costs.

Another study utilizing this technique (Rowan et al., 1961) dealt only with operating and maintenance costs of sewage treatment plants. The analysis included data from 321 treatment plants on four different processes: primary treatment (PT), standard-rate trickling filters (SRTF), high-rate trickling filters (HRTF), and activated sludge treatment (AS). Data were requested for the years 1955 through 1958 and averaged to determine the representative costs from each plant. This procedure was an attempt to correct for the possibility that a single cross-sectional cost observation from an individual plant may be biased if the plant has not adjusted to its designed capacity at that point in time.

The best fit resulted from using the following functional form:

$$\log y = \frac{1}{a + b \log x},$$

where y is the annual cost per unit of capacity and x is a measure of capacity. Two measures of capacity were used in this report: average daily flow in millions of gallons per day $\times$ 100, and population served $\times$ 0.01. The curves were fitted by ordinary least squares. The results of the regression are shown in Table 10.

Construction and operating costs for wastewater treatment plants were derived in another study (Logan et al., 1962). In this study the treatment of wastewater was divided into its unit processes, including preliminary treatment, primary treatment, secondary treatment, sludge handling, chlorination, sewage pumping, and administrative costs. The field data came from visits to plants and interviews with consulting engineers, and covered sixty-one plants. The results for construction costs of a primary treatment facility are summarized in Table

TABLE 10

Estimated annual sewage treatment plant operating and maintenance costs

Type of treatment	$/MGD	$/Capita
Primary	$\log y = 1 / (0.49273 + 0.23867 \log x)$	$\log y = 1 / (0.53161 + 0.16975 \log x)$
Activated sludge	$\log y = 1 / (0.40662 + 0.17223 \log x)$	$\log y = 1 / (0.40927 + 0.13791 \log x)$
Standard-rate filter	$\log y = 1 / (0.10405 + 0.43509 \log x)$	$\log y = 1 / (0.39745 + 0.24904 \log x)$
High-rate filter	$\log y = 1 / (0.36435 + 0.25968 \log x)$	$\log y = 1 / (0.32302 + 0.27926 \log x)$

SOURCE: Rowan, Jenkins, and Howells, 1961

TABLE 11

Field construction costs for primary treatment plant

Unit process subdivision	Unit process costs
Preliminary treatment	$16800 \ X^{-0.148}$
Primary treatment	$49300 \ X^{-0.104}$
Sludge handling	$117000 \ X^{-0.277}$
Total (incl. sludge handling)	$185000 \ X^{-0.201}$
Total (incl. chlorination and pumping)	$215000 \ X^{-0.210}$
Administrative and general	$78000 \ X^{-0.306}$
Total	$315000 \ X^{-0.245}$

NOTE: X is design capacity in millions of gallons per day
SOURCE: Logan, Hatfield, Russell, and Lynn, 1962.

11. Similar results were also derived for standard and high rate trickling filter plants as well as activated sludge plants.

Because of inconsistencies in some of the field data it was also decided to develop cost estimates based on theoretical designs for various processes. The unit construction costs derived in this way compared very well with the results derived using ordinary least squares on the field data.

Downing (1969) summarized one of the few attempts to relate annual sewage treatment costs to abatement efficiency (Frankel, 1965). In this report the costs of fifty-one alternative treatment plant designs at three capacities were estimated. The alternatives ranged fron chlorination only, to the most advanced tertiary treatment. Capital and operating costs, as well as suspended solids and BOD removal efficiencies, were estimated. A trend line was then fitted to the relationship between costs and removal for each of the three capacities. The marginal cost of abatement function was also derived (Downing, 1969, 36-72).

While statistical cost functions incorporate a theoretically superior methodology to that of engineering cost studies several important problems affect their reliability. One such problem is that the proper data often cannot be collected at a reasonable cost. The major problems with data that have been generated are that they may not represent a plant which has completely adjusted to its designed efficiency or capacity, and they are often biased, purposedly or accidentally, by emitters. Sometimes emitters are asked to allocate joint costs, which must often be arbitrary. At other times responses are purposely biased because of the fear that this data will be employed for regulatory purposes.

3 / Systems-approach cost studies

It appears that, at least for the present, the data restrictions reduce any advantage statistical techniques have over engineering studies. On the other hand the defects of engineering studies, in terms of rejecting all alternative substitution possibilities, is of major concern. The answer to this dilemma may be a systems approach to the derivation of abatement-cost functions. The systems approach entails defining an abatement production function in terms of all the alternative abatement techniques and then minimizing the cost of reaching any level of abatement subject to this production function.

Logan (1962) suggested this method in a study dealing with the economics of wastewater treatment. Because of inconsistencies in observed field data, cost estimates were made of a series of theoretical designs. All of these plants were theoretically located in St Louis in 1960 and assumed to treat average domestic effluent having a five-day BOD of 200mg/litre. Thirty four standard units[19] were designed and their construction costs estimated. Annual operating costs were based on field data. Annual capital costs were based on a twenty-year life and a 4 per cent rate of interest. With this method the most economic design could be chosen for any level of abatement. If the required BOD reduction was 85 per cent, systems analysis, through some form of linear or non-linear programming, could determine what combination of the above designed units could achieve this result most economically.

A slightly different methodology was incorporated into a study of abatement in the pulp and paper industry (Ecker and McNamara, 1971). This study assumed several abatement designs made up of individual processes in series. For example, one of the ten alternate designs considered was a primary clarifier (PC),

---

19 These 'units' are the component parts that make up the design of a wastewater treatment plant.

trickling filter plus activated sludge/secondary clarifier (TF + AS), and carbon absorption. The costs of the individual processes considered were presented in the following form: $Z = Ax_i^{-k}$, where Z is total annual costs ($1000) and x_i is the fraction of five-day BOD remaining in the effluent.

The design problem is to choose one of the ten alternate designs and the appropriate process levels to minimize the annual cost of achieving a certain level of abatement. By varying the required level of abatement and repeating the algorithm one could generate a cost-of-abatement function.

This study used geometric programming to minimize the annual costs of achieving a given level of abatement for all ten designs. The least-cost method can then be chosen by inspection, which also incidentally defines the level at which each process should be operated.

A more sophisticated approach to this methodology is presented in a study deriving the costs of abating fly-ash with an electrostatic precipitator (Watson, 1974). While this study does not allow for substitution of techniques for abating fly-ash (particulates), O'Connor and Citarella (1970) point out that electrostatic precipitators are the dominant technology for the abatement of particulates from power plant boilers. Therefore the derivation of an abatement-cost function for an electrostatic precipitator would in this case be a good proxy for the particulate abatement-cost function of a thermal power plant.[20]

Watson first estimated a theoretical precipitator efficiency function econometrically. He then formulated a structure and power plant input accounting cost equation ($SPAC_t$) in terms of the variables which appeared in the efficiency function. Minimizing $SPAC_t$, discounted at 8 per cent over thirty years, subject to the efficiency function, yields a total discounted power and structure cost equation (DPSC). By substituting into this equation the appropriate values we can determine the DPSC for a 1000 MW plant. Adding other costs, including those of maintenance and labour, additional fan operation, and fly-ash disposal, all properly discounted, we derive the total discounted cost in 1967 dollars of precipitating fly-ash from a representative 1000 MW unit:

$$DPC = 1{,}794{,}100 \left[\log n \left(100/100\text{-}Ep\right)\right]^{\frac{1}{2}} + 21130\,Ep + 1{,}018{,}656,$$

where DPC is total discounted costs in dollars, Ep is precipitator efficiency in percentage and n is the number of years of operation of the precipitation. 'An

20 Watson (1974, 168) notes that the only relevant technology currently available for fly-ash abatement is electrostatic precipitators either alone or with mechanical collectors in tandem. For efficiencies above 85 per cent electrostatic precipitators alone are the least-cost alternative (ibid., 169-73).

advantage of this methodology, in comparison with traditional purely statistical cost analysis, is that it brings more information to the analysis, thereby allowing more efficient estimation of model parameters' (Watson, 1974, 171).

Anderson (1970) suggested using this method of constrained cost minimization as a check on the statistically estimated cost function. He also presented a technique for pooling the systems-analysis and statistical cost curve to improve the properties of the model. Anderson concluded: 'Engineering information thus gives one kind of clairvoyance, an ability to see beyond the confines of what is frequently a very limited sample' (402).

4 / Summary
The three types of cost study distinguished in this section to a certain extent complement each other. Where data are available and technical knowledge is sufficient[21] the best results can be achieved by deriving both a statistical cost function and a systems-approach cost curve. However, where historical data points are subject to some doubt or where, as is often the case, these data points vary over a narrow range, the systems approach can help to develop a more realistic cost relationship. Best cost estimates for the abatement of sulphur dioxide, particulates, and BOD in 1974 dollars are presented in Table 12.

Additional problems in formulating and estimating costs
Other problems in deriving social abatement-cost functions include the treatment of taxes, the possible divergence between private and social costs, and uncertainty.

1 / Taxes
The social cost of abatement should include only allocative or opportunity costs. These costs are measured by the value that the resources used for abatement could have produced elsewhere in the economy. If the tax on abatement equipment is a general expenditure tax the market cost inclusive of the tax should be used to reflect opportunity cost, since the social value of any alternative product that could have been produced would include this tax. However, if the tax in question is specific only to abatement equipment it should not be included in the formulation of social costs. Similarly, subsidies specific to abatement equipment should be netted out of social cost calculations (Hartle, 1974, 17-18).

---

21 The constrained minimization techniques used by Anderson and Watson require the derivation of an engineering production function. This is not always possible, and even where it is, it generally requires extensive technical knowledge.

TABLE 12

Estimated costs of pollution abatement

Pollutant removed	Removal efficiency (%)	Equipment or process	Kind and size of plant	Capital costs	Operating and maintenance costs	Total annual costs	Annual cost per unit of pollutant removed
Sulphur dioxide[a] (SO_2)	90	Limestone scrubbing	Thermal power plant (200 MW)	$50/KW	N	0.9-1.8 mills/KWH	$0.033-0.066/lb of SO_2 removed[b]
Biochemical oxygen demand (BOD)	95	Activated sludge	Sewage treatment plant (10mgd)	$574,000/mgd[c]	$19,725/mgd[d]	$707,000[e]	$0.09/lb of BOD removed[f]
Particulates	98	Electrostatic precipitator	Thermal power plant (1000MW)	N	N	$600,000[g]	$0.001/lb of particulate removed[b]

NOTE: All costs converted to fourth quarter 1974 dollars using the Implicit Price Index (business gross fixed capital formation). (Statistics Canada, 62-002, Jan. 1975, 87)

a Slack, Falkinberry, and Harrington, 1972
b Assuming: coal burned has a sulphur content of 2.35%; an ash content of 10.15%; power plant thermal efficiency is 35%; 12,500 British Thermal Units (BTU) per ton of coal; 3413 BTU per KWH; and a load factor of 54.4%

c Logan, Hatfield, Russell, and Lynn, 1962
d Rowan, Jenkins, and Howells, 1961
e Discounting over a 30-year period at 8%
f Assuming an average concentration of BOD of 300 ppm. (parts per million)
g Watson, 1974

2 / Divergence between private and social costs

Unemployed resources. In cases where market prices do not reflect the social costs of certain inputs shadow prices should be derived. If, for example, an abatement project were to employ a unit of previously idle productive ability (i.e. either a unit of labour or capital), the cost of that unit, which would otherwise have been idle, should be below the market price.[22] This allowance, however, only applies to the initial period. Thereafter, it should be assumed that full employment again prevails and the resources should be valued at the prevailing market rate (Arrow, 1965).

Amenity costs. The monetary costs of abatement in certain circumstances may not properly measure the social costs of abatement (ibid.). For example, if the limestone slurry generated by limestone scrubbing of flue gases to remove sulphur oxides were dumped into a nearby river, polluting it, the social cost of this pollution should be assigned a value and included among the costs of abating sulphur oxides.

Social discount rate. The discount rate is used to translate future costs and benefits into present values. The relevant social rate has been the subject of much controversy. Two alternative methods of calculation can be distinguished (Haveman, 1969). First, the opportunity cost approach adopts the position that no investment should be undertaken which produces output of less value than the alternative uses of the resources it absorbs. The discount methodology suggested in the discussion above of control-cost categories corresponds to such a position. Second, the social rate of time preference approach recognizes that privately appropriable gains and costs on which individuals base their decisions about consumption, savings, and investment do not adequately reflect social benefits and costs. This is so because private decisions based as they are on market rates of interest, ignore future generations. Proponents of this approach, which is identified with conservationists, opt for a lower rate of discount than advocates of the opportunity cost approach.

It is probably impossible to determine which approach is correct. However, a technique has been suggested for circumscribing the problem: 'The inevitable subjectiveness in choice of a social discount rate provides an instance where the use of sensitivity analysis may be advisable, to test whether the conclusions of an evaluation are affected greatly by the choice of a particular discount rate' (Hartle, 1974, 30).

Dislocation costs. Thus far we have ignored the possibility that a firm may go out of business if abatement costs are an excessive burden. This possibility may

22 Arrow (1965) says that the social cost of the otherwise idle labourer is zero. This ignores the utility the individual receives from leisure and fails to incorporate it as a social opportunity cost.

represent significant short-run costs, especially for an individual jurisdiction. In such a case, at the critical abatement level the marginal social cost of abatement will become much steeper than if the firm continued in operation. Even if a firm remains in business, increased abatement may result in layoffs and unemployment, and significant social costs may be involved with this transitional unemployment in the short run, but not in the long run. These costs should be included along with firm abatement-costs to determine social abatement-costs.

3 / Uncertainty

We may consider two types of uncertainty: statistical uncertainty and uncertainty with respect to future states of the world (Hartle, 1974). Statistical uncertainty stems from chance elements, and a technique for dealing with it has been suggested by Ezzati (1974). The other type of uncertainty, however, is more troublesome, and it has been suggested that the use of sensitivity analysis could help in dealing with it. Sensitivity analysis tells how sensitive the cost model is to changes in values of key variables, such as discount rate and future relative input prices. This procedure helps in evaluating the significance of certain key assumptions.

SUMMARY AND CONCLUSIONS

The cost of abatement processes can be defined as a function of the capacity of abatement equipment or of the waste removal efficiency of the process. If it is derived to determine optimal levels of pollution the relevant concept is the cost-abatement relationship. Although many sources in the literature define the cost capacity functions for various levels of abatement, they can be easily transformed to the cost-abatement relationship.

The polluter has many alternative techniques of abating pollution, including treatment of wastes, varying input mix, and reducing output. These should all be considered when deriving a cost-of-abatement function. Each method should be used up to the point at which the marginal cost of waste reduction by each alternative is equal.

In general, the firm will not consider the alternative of increasing environmental assimilative capacity. This should be taken into account in any socially optimal program of abatement.

The cost components generally used in the various studies of cost-abatement relationships are capital investment costs, operating and maintenance costs, and annual capital costs. Annual capital costs are made up of interest, taxes, insurance, and depreciation. Of these categories the interest and depreciation costs are the most controversial. The 'correct' interest rate, which defines the firm's opportunity cost of investing in abatement equipment, depends on whether the firm is a borrower or lender. Depreciation should be included in total capital costs through the use of the annuity bond method. Total annual costs can be determined by adding operating and maintenance costs to annual capital costs.

Control-cost studies can be divided into three classes: engineering studies, statistical cost studies, and systems-approach cost studies. The engineering studies are concerned mainly with tail-end abatement techniques. Many of these studies dwell at length on capital investment costs with operating and maintenance costs treated arbitrarily. These studies list the capital equipment necessary to achieve a certain abatement goal under specified conditions. The cost of this equipment is then summed to determine over-all capital investment costs. The drawbacks of many engineering studies are that they do not allow for substitution of all alternative abatement methods in deriving costs and that very often these studies only derive single-point cost estimates. Certain studies have tried to remedy this last defect (US, 1969b; Ezzati, 1974) by deriving confidence intervals in place of these point estimates. Still another approach (Dewees, 1974; Brandt and Mann, 1973) has been to use various engineering point-cost estimates and fit trend lines to represent the abatement-cost relationship.

Statistical cost studies in most cases consist of fitting cost-abatement or cost-capacity relationships with the aid of statistical techniques. The major problems with them relate to the reliability and meaning of the data. If a firm is not in long-run equilibrium when the observation for the cost relationship is made, the results will be biased. The reliability question stems from the possibility that suppliers of the information, notably the firms using the equipment, may fear that the information will be used for regulatory purposes.

The systems-analysis studies attempt to minimize the cost of abatement subject to a production function of emission reductions that considers large numbers of alternative units or processes. The input data for this approach come largely from engineering studies. One author has even suggested a combination of the systems-analysis approach and statistical derivation (Anderson, 1970).

Finally, when formulating and estimating social abatement costs one must consider the incorporation of taxes, the determination of relevant social costs, and allowances for uncertainty.

5
Monitoring and information cost

Most of the economics literature on externalities and their control has assumed that it is possible to determine at zero cost precisely what is released into the environment and by whom. This assumption is carried over from other areas of economics where the relevant variables are of necessity already measured by individuals, firms, or government for internal business or tax purposes. In the case of income, revenues, and expenditures, it is usually correct to assume that measurement has already been made. In the case of pollution emissions, however, the opposite is true. In the absence of any pollution regulations, most firms make few or no measurements of their discharges into the environment. Governments rarely measure emissions unless this is part of a specific pollution control program. The cost of such measurement is too great to be borne unless there is a direct need for the results. A frequent problem in establishing effective pollution control programs is that an effective scheme of monitoring and surveillance is too expensive for the enforcement agency to bear. Thus it is important to look more closely at the costs of measurement as they relate to environmental policies, to discover how these costs affect the choice of policy.

Thus far we have discussed the problems of measuring the quantity of effluent discharged into the environment. Another measurement problem in some ways may be more important for environmental policies. This is the difficulty of measuring costs and benefits that would result from a proposed policy or that have resulted as a result of existing policies. The chapters above on benefits and costs of pollution control have dealt at some length with the problem of estimating or forecasting these variables. Since some determination of costs and benefits must be made for any environmental policy, the expense of this determination is a factor in choosing among policies. We shall assume that any pollution problems to be considered in this study are sufficiently serious to warrant some expenditure to derive estimates of benefits and costs and therefore of an appropriate degree of control. This chapter therefore concentrates exclusively on the costs of monitoring emissions and enforcing whatever policy is adopted. Methods and costs of determining emission rates are reviewed, and the role that measurements play in alternative pollution control policies are examined. Noting that different policies use monitoring information for quite different purposes and therefore have different needs, we study how the cost of monitoring and enforcement can affect the choice of pollution control policies. Finally, we address the question who should bear the costs of effluent monitoring. Not only is this an efficiency issue, the large costs associated with monitoring programs render decisions about who must finance them important in terms of distribution and equity.

METHODS OF MEASUREMENT

The rate of pollution emission by a firm is generally determined by a number of factors, including the type of capital equipment used in the process, the maintenance of production and emission control equipment, operating methods and inputs, and the rate of product output. The latter may vary seasonally, daily, even hourly. Thus emission rates may be subject to substantial variations during periods as short as an hour. If the production process involves batch operations, which discharge pollutants when the batch is emptied or the vat cleaned, emissions may vary widely from one minute to the next.

In some cases operation and maintenance procedures may have little effect on the rate of emissions. Where this is the case it may be possible to estimate emissions accurately by determining the characteristics of the capital equipment and noting the total input or output from the production process. For example, few fossil fuel power plants employ devices for removing sulphur dioxide from stack gases, so that a reasonably constant proportion of all sulphur in a fuel goes up the stack. Total emissions of sulphur dioxide from a fossil fuel fired boiler could therefore be determined accurately from the sulphur content of the fuel (which any major fuel user would have determined in advance) and the quantity of fuel consumed. In such a case the measurement problem becomes almost trivial. Testing the capital equipment to determine its average rate of emission per unit of input or output is all that is necessary. The firm need only state the quantities of inputs (coal burned) or outputs (electricity generated) and the pollution content of the fuel for the control authority to determine emissions precisely.

When operating and maintenance procedures may significantly affect the rate of emission, examination of the capital equipment can no longer determine the emission rate adequately, and it becomes necessary to rely on some form of direct measurement. The most common type of direct measurement program is statistical or periodic effluent sampling, by which the rate of discharge or the density of discharge is measured from time to time. Sometimes this monitoring is on a scheduled or announced basis. Where it is possible to make short-run adjustments in the production or pollution control process that significantly affect the rate of emissions, such a program can lead to biased estimates of average emission rates if the polluter prepares for the measurements by reducing all variable emission components. It is therefore more common to sample on a random, unannounced basis.

In the case of water pollution, three types of measurement are available. The grab sample is the least expensive and the easiest to apply. The testing officer inserts a cup or bucket into the discharge stream and sends the contents to a laboratory to be tested. Since it usually takes only a few seconds to fill the container the sample represents an insignificant portion of even one day's effluent, much less the effluent of the month or two that frequently separates samples. If the emission rate changes significantly on a short-term basis the standard error of the sample mean of grab samples may be quite high. Frequently the variance of individual grab sample measurements of biochemical oxygen demand (BOD) or suspended solids (SS) may be as great as the mean of those measurements. Clearly a large number of such measurements would be needed to determine an emission rate with sufficient accuracy that an effluent charge or emission rights scheme could be based upon it.

A partial attack on this problem is possible with a composite sampler. This machine can be temporarily placed in the outfall and will take a small sample of discharge water every hour for up to twenty-four hours. All samples are placed in a single container which thus holds the contents of up to twenty-four grab samples. This obviously provides far more information than the single grab sample, and the variance of composite sample observations about the mean is substantially less than the variation of grab sample observations. Still more detailed information can be gathered with the sequential sampler, which takes up to twenty-four samples on an hourly basis but maintains them separately for individual testing. Equipment that performs similar functions is available for some types of air pollution monitoring.

Table 13 shows some statistical properties of effluent density measurements of three industrial firms subject to the sewer surcharge in London, Ontario. Firms 6 and 7 were subjected to both composite sampling and grab samples. At least twenty measurements were made for each entry. As expected, the standard

TABLE 13

Statistical properties of effluent measurements

Firm	Sample type	Pollutant	Mean value (μ)	Standard deviation (σ)	$\dfrac{\sigma}{\mu}$	Percentage within one standard deviation of mean		
						Above and below	Above only	Below only
6	C	BOD	880	514	0.58	74	37	37
	C	SS	642	257	0.40	70	26	44
6	G	BOD	1764	1583	0.90	86	18	68
	G	SS	1510	990	0.65	86	25	61
7	C	BOD	2819	1890	0.67	60	10	50
	C	SS	2436	2449	1.0	88	17	61
7	G	BOD	3650	2794	0.77	86	23	63
	G	SS	2468	2932	1.19	91	26	65
9	C	BOD	1842	1486	0.81	89	22	67
	C	SS	391	379	0.97	91	22	69

NOTE: C is composite samples usually over twenty-four hours; G is grab sample
SOURCE: Analysis of industrial monitoring data from London, Ontario

deviation of the grab samples for both pollution measures is a larger percentage of the mean than is the standard deviation of the composite samples. This suggests that substantial variations in effluent density take place within a twenty-four-hour period. In all cases, for BOD and SS the standard deviation divided by the mean (σ/μ) is at least 0.4, and in 80 per cent of the measurements it is over 0.65. This means that many measurements are necessary to establish a mean emission rate with any precision. Of course not all of this variation is random; some is probably related to rates of product output or other variables that could be observed directly. Tests for time trend, seasonal variation, and water use, however, had no significant explanatory power.

The shape of the distribution was examined by testing the percentage of all observations within one standard deviation on each side of the mean. In general, a greater share of the BOD and SS readings were below than above, suggesting a distribution skewed to the right, with the mode and median below the mean. This is a natural result of a distribution bounded from below but with no practicable limit on the maximum pollution density.

Sims and Amborski (1974) report that the province of Ontario monitors the effluent discharge of a number of firms from one to four times annually, depending on size. The city of London, Ontario, is one of several cities to institute a sewer surcharge upon polluters emitting wastes that exceed specified concentration standards into the municipal sewage system. Firms in that city are subjected to a twenty-four-hour composite measurement varying in interval from every few months to every two weeks. This practice suggests the frequency deemed necessary to provide data with sufficient accuracy for levying an effluent charge.

The costs of such monitoring programs are substantial. It has been reported that gathering a field sample may cost fifty dollars per visit. Testing that sample can cost from five to fifteen dollars per parameter tested, with some complex parameters costing far more. Thus a single sample tested for five parameters could cost one hundred dollars. The province of Ontario collected over seven thousand water pollution samples in 1972 alone.

The logical extension of statistical or periodic sampling is continuous monitoring of a source of discharge. This could be accomplished by a series of twenty-four-hour sequential or composite samples taken with no pause between. Because the laboratory testing costs of such a program would be enormous, this should only be undertaken at sources of major problems.

ROLE OF MEASUREMENT IN ENVIRONMENTAL POLICIES

Selection of a sampling program will depend not only on the characteristics of the pollution-producing process but also on the policy being enforced. If the regulation is imposed by an effluent charge, monitoring need only produce an accurate long-term average measure of effluent quantity and concentration. If a reasonably accurate average emission rate can be established, this may be multiplied by the time period to produce total emissions, a figure forming the basis for the effluent charge. The same requirements apply for an effluent-rights system such as that proposed by Dales (1968). Here the limitation is not on discharge at any moment but the total discharge over a day, a month, or a year. Once again, determination of an accurate average emission rate can be used to estimate total emissions.

If the abatement policy is an absolute prohibition against emissions that exceed some standard, however, it is necessary to determine, not the average quantity and quality of discharge, but whether a specified level has ever been exceeded even for a short period of time. Courts of law will not accept probabilistic inferences that a violation must have occurred because the average emissions are close to the absolute standard. To prove a violation in court it is necessary to have actually observed a violation of the standard. If a polluter is to be caught and convicted for a large percentage of the occasions when his emissions exceed the standard, it is necessary to make measurements frequently within the time period over which those emissions can change substantially. Thus an absolute standard may require a greater volume of data and more frequent sampling than the enforcement of an effluent charge or emission rights scheme.

To understand arguments about frequency of monitoring, one must examine how measurements are used to enforce a policy. Consider a situation in which the polluter's behaviour is not affected by arguments or pressure, but only by actual costs imposed on him. The efficient degree of abatement will be reached when the marginal cost of abatement is equal to the marginal benefits. The profit-maximizing polluter will abate until his marginal abatement cost equals his marginal penalties. Optimality requires that the marginal penalties imposed on the polluter for any increase in his emissions must equal marginal benefits.

Under an emission standard the penalties assessed against the polluter will depend upon the frequency with which he is caught and the magnitude of the fine. If the fine for violating a standard is roughly related to the damage caused by that violation, which would seem to satisfy a judicial sense of equity, a large percentage of violations must result in convictions if the fines imposed are to approximate the social cost of pollution. While there are many examples of fines in excess of the damage (such as a fifty-dollar littering fine), there is clearly a conflict between deterrence and equity. If the polluter's emission rate is subject to some significant variations, the more frequently his effluent is monitored the more frequently he can be caught and convicted. For a given effluent standard, the higher his average rate of emission the more often he is likely to be in violation and therefore likely to be caught.

Figure 13 plots the cost to the polluter of being convicted under an effluent standard system as a function of his emission rate and the variance in his emissions. If the variance in his emission rate is small (curve A) there will be no cost until he is close to the standard, and costs will rise rapidly as he reaches or exceeds the standard. On the other hand, if the variance in his emission rate is high he will begin to incur costs long before his mean rate reaches the standard. The slope of the cost-to-polluter function will be less steep than if the variance in emissions is small (curve A'). With a high variance in the emission rate the cost of emissions as a function of the average emission rate is rather like that in the case of an effluent charge, or perhaps an effluent surcharge with an allowable free amount. The more you emit, the more you pay.

We can also plot the effect of varying monitoring frequency on the expected cost to the polluter of his emissions under a standard-and-fine system. The probability of being caught in violation is proportional to the percentage of time that the polluter is in violation and the percentage of time that monitoring takes place. For a given mean emission rate, then, the cost to the polluter will be proportional to the number of measurements. If curves A and A' in Figure 13

Figure 13
Expected cost of emissions with standard and fine
(n is number of measurements; σ is the variance of sample emission
rates about the mean emission rate. From Dewees, 1973)

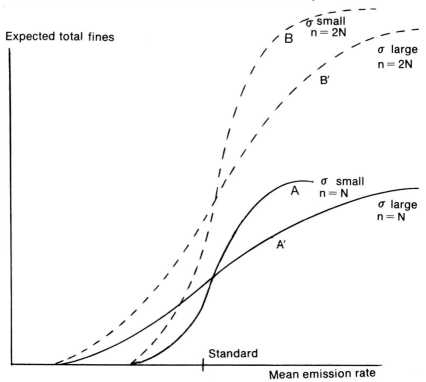

represent a measurement frequency of N, a measurement frequency of $2N$ will produce curves B and B'. For any emission rate, the cost is doubled. Thus, increasing the fine and increasing the monitoring frequency are substitute means of increasing costs to the polluter.

Under an effluent charge system the effect of monitoring frequency on the polluter's costs is quite different from the standard-and-fine system. The samples are used to determine a mean emission rate that is then translated into total emissions for the period. The frequency of measurement should not affect the estimate of the mean emission rate, except to change its precision. The more frequently the polluter is monitored, the more accurately his emission rate can be estimated. Since there is no particular reason for upward or downward bias in an estimate the expected cost to the polluter should not change significantly as the number of measurements is increased or decreased. All that changes is the accuracy with which the sample estimates the actual rate. If we look at the relationship between the average rate of emission and the total effluent charge paid, it should be a straight line running through the origin. Since the frequency of monitoring does not affect the cost imposed on the polluter it does not affect his equilibrium rate of emission. Thus the frequency of monitoring can be chosen solely with regard to balancing monitoring costs against precision of measurement.

The case of an emission rights policy is identical to that of an effluent charge. Since it is only necessary to determine the mean rate over a period, more frequent measurements simply increase the accuracy of the estimate, they do not change the cost of the program to the polluter. Again, the frequency of measurement will be selected with regard to balancing monitoring costs against inaccuracy of measurement.

But with a given monitoring frequency it is possible to design a standard-and-fine system that yields marginal costs to the polluter similar to those of an effluent charge. If the effluent charge only applies to emissions in excess of some base amount, the cost to the polluter is a sloping straight line intersecting the horizontal axis at the base amount. If the fine is made proportional to the degree to which the standard is exceeded, the fine system will produce similar results. The line will be non-linear (because of the variance in emission rates), but its slope can be made to approach that of the effluent charge. The standard and the charge, if properly designed, can thus be used for similar purposes.

A fundamental difference appears, however, between an effluent standard and an effluent charge scheme in the design of a monitoring policy. In a standard scheme, frequency of monitoring will directly affect the cost imposed on the polluter, and therefore the average emission rate he selects. In the case of an effluent charge or effluent rights program, frequency of measurement affects only precision. Thus the equilibrium rate of emission for the polluter does not depend significantly upon measurement costs.

CHOICE OF POLICY

From the above information on measurement costs in various programs some conclusions can be drawn regarding the impact of measurement costs on a pollution control program. If the source of pollution is such that the emission rate can be determined accurately from an examination of the capital equipment used, measurement is not really a problem. Available makes and models of equipment can be tested and rated to determine whether or not they meet some standard. Their emission rate can be estimated so that when combined with input or output information it could be used as a basis for an effluent charge or emission rights program. In any event the measurement cost will be small.

Where direct monitoring of the discharge is necessary, measurement costs can be an important element in selecting the proper policy. If the pollution control program is a serious one, significant action being taken against many polluters to achieve the desired reduction in ambient pollution concentrations, a significant amount of monitoring will be necessary.

In the case of an effluent standard, where the fine is reasonably related to the damage done from a single discharge, sampling must be frequent enough to catch a high percentage of all violations. If an effluent charge program or an effluent rights program is used against the same polluters, it is only necessary to make sufficient measurements to accurately estimate an average emission rate. In most cases this should require less frequent measurements than an emission standards program. For a serious program the monitoring cost should therefore be less with an effluent charge or effluent rights scheme than with an effluent standard.

It is frequently argued, however, that effluent charge programs are impractical because the monitoring expenditures are too great. This argument is made by those in charge of pollution control programs who should be knowledgeable in these matters. Still, it may be possible to reconcile these protests with the above analysis. In some cases compliance with a standard is achieved, not by monitoring and conviction in court, but by persuasion and veiled threats. The monitoring program is only sufficient to determine which polluters must be near or above the standard, and the agency works with those polluters until they install proper equipment and adopt operating procedures likely to bring the emission rate below the standard. When this procedure is used the monitoring program need only determine the mean emission rate. Thus it may be no more expensive than that for an effluent charge, and perhaps even less expensive since the evaluation is a subjective one.

In other cases, especially when many polluters are well below the standard, effluent standards are adopted without providing the administrative machinery necessary to seriously enforce them. If few sources are likely to be in violation of the standard, very little monitoring is necessary. Even when many polluters are near or above the standard, if there is no serious intention of enforcement it is easy to perform few measurements and thus keep costs low. In either of these cases there will be little reduction in emissions, but there will also be minimal monitoring costs. When an effluent charge is proposed in such a situation it invariably increases monitoring costs greatly, since any polluter could legitimately protest against a charge based on few or no measurements. In short, if a program is not intended to have much affect, an effluent standard will be cheaper than an effluent charge. If the program is serious and if conviction for violations is to be the primary enforcement for reduced emissions, monitoring costs in most cases should be lower for an effluent charge program.

ASSIGNING THE MEASUREMENT COST BURDEN

The discussion so far has assumed that all monitoring is performed by the regulatory agency responsible for pollution control. There is no reason, however, why individual pollution sources could not be compelled to monitor themselves. One could require every source of pollution to perform measurements on a regular basis and submit statements on the quantities or densities of pollution measured. A government agency could audit these returns and perform random measurements to ascertain that the filed statements were generally accurate. Such a procedure would be analogous to that used for collecting income tax. The burden is on the individual or firm to keep its own records, and make statements of tax liability to the authorities, while random audits of individual and corporate returns provide an incentive to honesty. A similar scheme for pollution monitoring seems feasible.

The effect of such a program would be to shift the financial burden of effluent monitoring from the government to the polluter. Some cost reductions might follow, such as lower transportation costs for the monitoring personnel. On the other hand, small firms might hire consultants to do their monitoring, a practice that could result in costs quite similar to those of a government agency. Monitoring should be paid for by the firms whenever the optimum number of measurements is a function of the emission variance. In such cases a firm, knowing that measurement requirements would be smaller if it reduced its discharge variance, would weigh such savings against the cost of making emissions more uniform. If the government paid for the monitoring, or if monitoring requirements were set non-optimally, firms would consider only the fines or charges to which they were subject and neglect the impact of their decisions on monitoring costs.

An equally important question may be the allocation of this burden between the private and public sector. It should probably be resolved in individual jurisdictions, depending upon the technical competence of private and government personnel and the funds available to the government agency.

CONCLUSIONS

While the design of monitoring programs for various pollution policies has received little attention from economists, the cost of adequate measurement and the limits imposed by imperfect measurement are major factors in the selection and success of pollution control policies. The high cost of discharge sampling sometimes leads to emission estimates based on capital equipment alone, which biases control strategies towards capital intensive solutions and away from operating and maintenance expense. High monitoring costs mean that only a small percentage of all violations of an effluent standard can be detected, so that fines must be many times the actual damage from the emissions to achieve optimal abatement. And where the variation in emission rates over time is substantial, even an effluent charge requires numerous measurements to establish a fair basis for the charge.

While it is often alleged that an effluent charge requires more expensive monitoring than an effluent standard, this is difficult to demonstrate with reasonable models. The effluent charge requires a sufficient number of measurements to estimate accurately a mean emission rate. The effluent standard requires enough measurements to detect a significant proportion of all violations of the standard. Even if there are substantial variations in the emission rate, the standard could require a higher number of measurements than the charge.

It is clear, however, that the entire field of discharge monitoring requires further study. It is essential to gather good statistical descriptions of discharge rates and test a variety of monitoring strategies to determine their performance under alternative control policies. Much further theoretical and empirical work will be necessary to improve the cost/effectiveness of current monitoring programs.

6
Evaluation of control policies

In the second chapter we noted that environmental problems can be divided between cases where negotiation between the polluter and pollutee is possible and those where it is not. In the former, because there are few parties on both sides, Coase (1960) demonstrated that the parties could reach an efficient control of pollution and allocation of resources through negotiation subject to the legislated allocation of environmental rights. However, most major environmental problems could not possibly be solved by negotiation because too many parties are involved. This chapter will focus on problems and remedies for situations in which negotiation is not possible and government action is necessary to avoid a serious misallocation of resources. The question is: what form should this government action take? We shall consider policy alternatives in three categories and evaluate their characteristics in a variety of situations.

STANDARDS, PRICES, AND RIGHTS

The primary pollution regulation instrument in the past has been a pollution standard specifying a maximum lawful rate of emissions. For some time, however, economists have recommended the use of prices or effluent charges to regulate emissions. And, more recently, a market system of pollution rights has been proposed, sharing many of the desirable characteristics of effluent charges (Dales 1968).

Emission standards
Emission standards specify the maximum rate at which pollutants may be discharged into the air or water. They must be distinguished from ambient

quality standards, which specify an environmental quality goal for the water body or airshed. Whether or not an ambient standard is met depends upon the emissions from all relevant polluters and the dispersion of pollutants in the area. While ambient standards can set environmental goals in an area, they are not an enforcable regulation against a single polluter (this point is discussed below in the section on ambient standards).

An emission standard may specify the maximum allowable emissions in terms of absolute density, absolute total rate, or a quantity related to the activity in the production process. An example of a density regulation would be: 'subject to sub-sections 2 and 3, no persons shall cause or permit to be caused the emission of smoke having a density or opacity greater than density No. 1.'[1] Other emission standards may specify density in parts per million, grams per cubic metre, or some other measure of concentration. A regulation referring to density may provide an incentive to dilute the pollution with more air or water so that more sophisticated air pollution regulations limit the amount of artificial dilution permissible.

Another form of regulation ties the quantity of emissions to an input to or output of the production process. Thus, it may be prohibited to burn coal containing more than 1 per cent sulphur. Particulates may be limited to a certain number of pounds per ton of coal burned or per ton of cement produced. Alternatively, the regulation may limit total discharge from an outfall, stack, or plant, although this form is uncommon because under it a large operator can emit no more total pollution than a small one; it would provide an incentive to install more smoke stacks and outfalls, or to build multiple plants.

If pollution is thought of as use of the environment for disposal of wastes (a commodity not traded in a market) a system of effluent standards is like a rationing system for traded commodities. Under rationing the government specifies a quantity that may be consumed by each individual and distributes ration coupons free of charge. With pollution regulation the government specifies how much of the environment may be used by each firm and allows this use at no charge. As is sometimes the case in a rationing system, the distribution of rights under an effluent standard system is not uniform per capita but depends upon the polluter's activity or 'needs.' Thus many of the inefficiencies known to exist in rationing systems could also be expected with an effluent standard.

In general, effluent standards are applied uniformly for similarly situated polluters in an area. It would be far too expensive for a pollution control

1 Ontario Regulation 133/70, section 8(1). (Regulations made under the Ontario Air Pollution Control Act, 1967) Reprinted in Auld (1972).

Figure 14
Abatement cost with effluent standard

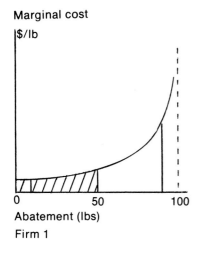

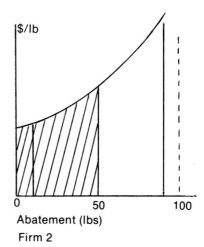

authority to gather cost and benefit information separately for each firm, except in the case of very large operations. Thus it is necessary to examine the effect of a uniform effluent standard on two dissimilar firms. Suppose that the two firms have marginal control costs as shown in Figure 14. Without pollution regulations, both firms emit one hundred pounds per day with zero abatement. If a uniform regulation prohibits emissions greater than fifty pounds per day, both firms must control fifty pounds per day, as shown in the figure. Because the abatement-cost curves are different, firm 1 experiences much lower marginal costs than firm 2. The total abatement cost for firm 1 is also much less than that for firm 2.

Effluent charge
An effluent charge is a price paid for discharging wastes into the environment. Generally such a charge is based, not upon density, but upon the total quantity of waste discharged. For example, a sewer authority might charge ten cents per pound of BOD discharged into the sewer system. Kneese and Bower (1968) discuss the characteristics and advantages of effluent charge schemes. They argue that imposing a price on waste discharge encourages the polluter to reduce the amount of discharge below the levels prevailing when it was free. Thus an effluent charge can be found which will give the same total pollution reduction as any emission standard.

Figure 15
Abatement cost with effluent charge

Marginal cost

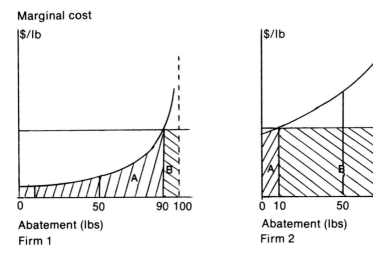

Firm 1

Firm 2

If an effluent charge that is uniform for the pollution problem area is imposed, all firms pay the same price per unit. Their response will be to control emissions until the marginal cost of further abatement is just equal to the effluent charge, so that all firms will arrive at an equal marginal abatement cost. This minimizes the total cost of pollution control. Figure 15 shows the behaviour of the two previously discussed firms operating under a uniform effluent charge. The charge has been designed so that the total pollution reduction for the two firms is one hundred pounds per day, the same as under the effluent standard. Firm 1 abates by ninety pounds per day and firm 2 by ten pounds per day for a total of one hundred. The cost incurred by each firm for pollution control is the shaded area A under its marginal cost curve. Clearly the total cost for the two firms under an effluent charge is lower than under the effluent standard, although the same total abatement is achieved. Thus the effluent charge achieves greater abatement efficiency.

In the case of an effluent charge, however, the total cost to the firm is not limited to its abatement cost; it must also pay for the pollution it still discharges. This payment is equal to the area under the effluent charge price to the right of the actual abatement line, shaded area B in Figure 15. The firm undertaking the most abatement pays the smallest total effluent charge. Clearly the total financial impact on the firms of the effluent charge is greater than that of the effluent standard, although the abatement cost itself is lower. For firm number 2 the burden of the effluent charge is greater even than its abatement cost would have been under an effluent standard.

A modified effluent charge is sometimes proposed to achieve the efficiency characteristics of the charge but to reduce its financial impact. Suppose that the effluent charge shown in Figure 15 represents ten cents per pound. We could respecify this to apply only to emissions in pounds per day in excess of ten for each polluter. In this case firm 1, which has reduced its emissions by ninety pounds, to ten pounds, would pay no effluent charge. Firm 2, which has reduced its emissions by ten pounds would pay for eighty of the remaining ninety pounds per day. By applying this 'free base discount' to the effluent charge we can reduce the financial impact on all firms while retaining the incentive to equalize marginal abatement costs. This discount should be applied to an emission level no greater than the smallest amount of pollution released by any firm. In this way it will not interfere with the marginal price paid by each firm. The different income effect of the discount will, however, yield different long-run effects because of the price effect.

Kneese and Bower (1968) suggest that a subsidy could achieve the same result as an effluent charge. If the polluter is paid a specified amount per unit for reducing his pollution the marginal gain to the polluter from any reduction is identical to his gain if he were paying a charge for each unit he emitted. Thus the marginal effect of a subsidy on pollution control must be identical to the marginal effect of a charge.

The subsidy, however, raises the problem of determining the base amount from which reductions will be computed for compensation. The pollution control authority must estimate what would have been emitted in the absence of the subsidy. This requires either static cost and demand curves over time or perfect information by the authority about the shape of those curves for every firm. Both assumptions are unrealistic and render subsidy schemes impractical, if not impossible.

Even if the information problem could be overcome subsidies raise two further problems which render their effects different from a charge. The effluent charge will increase costs, and thereby prices, for the polluting industry, yet a subsidy scheme that raises prices will cause high profits and encourage other firms to enter the industry. Of four sets of subsidy rules the only one that reduces pollution by the same amount as a charge would bankrupt the pollution control authority. The other three sets reduce emissions less than the equivalent effluent charge and leave product prices lower (Dewees and Sims, 1975). Social efficiency requires the price of polluting products to be greater than the price of similar products produced with less pollution, so that the subsidy scheme is not identical to a charge but clearly inferior.

While it is often said that an effluent charge can achieve an effect identical to any given direct regulation, the income and entry consequences of the two schemes must also be considered. Even if an effluent charge is set to achieve the same abatement as a standard, it will impose higher costs on the industry. With free entry and exit from the industry, this will yield higher product prices with the effluent charge, and consequently lower total output. If the charge produces the socially efficient allocation of resources, the environmentally equivalent standard is allocatively inefficient, not because it does not equate abatement-cost margins, but because it fails to extract payment for use of the environmental resource. If an effluent charge is efficient, a standard is not.

A frequently used form of subsidy has been government assistance for pollution control expenditures, through grants to cover capital investment in pollution control facilities or accelerated depreciation allowances for those facilities. Either scheme lowers the financial burden on a firm of reducing its emissions. Neither, however, causes the installation of pollution controls where none would have been installed otherwise. Since controls produce zero profit, making them free or nearly free is still not sufficient to cause their installation. Thus a tax relief or subsidy can reduce the impact of an effluent charge or effluent standard program, but it cannot cause pollution reduction by itself.

A further problem with these programs is that they almost always apply only to capital equipment. Subsidizing capital equipment, but not operating or maintenance costs, distorts the mix of capital and other inputs chosen for pollution control. This distortion must cause some increase in total pollution control costs (Bird and Waverman, 1972).

POLLUTION RIGHTS

Dales (1968) has suggested that instead of setting a price for using the environment and letting the marketplace decide how much use will be made of it, as in the case of effluent charges, we should set a total quantity of pollution discharge and allow the market to allocate that quantity among polluters and establish a price. We shall refer to the proposed scheme as the 'pollution rights' policy.

Suppose that one thousand pounds per day of BOD are discharged into a river. Suppose further that a control authority would like to reduce this to five hundred pounds per day. The authority would print certificates each allowing the holder to discharge one, ten, or one hundred pounds per day of BOD into the river with the total issue equalling five hundred pounds. The rights would be good for one year only. It would be unlawful to discharge BOD in access of the total amount of rights held by the polluter; thus, a polluter who expected to discharge two hundred pounds per day of BOD during 1975 would have to purchase two hundred pounds of 1975 BOD rights. Alternatively, the rights could have an infinite duration and be traded among polluters, or even leased from the authority.

The authority would hold an auction every year at which it would sell the right to discharge in the upcoming year. Polluters would bid against each other until the price per unit was reached at which all units were sold. During the year, as polluters changed their plans, they might offer unused rights for sale or bid for additional rights, so that after the first auction at which all rights are distributed there would be a continuing market for the unused portion of current rights. The price of a right would depend upon the total number issued and the demand for waste discharge.

Returning to the two firms of Figure 15, it should be clear that if rights for one hundred pounds per day were issued, the two firms would bid the price up to the level at which they would emit a combined total of one hundred pounds per day. The price of the rights would therefore be exactly the same as the effluent charge that led to the same total emissions. The pollution rights scheme shares all the efficiency characteristics of the effluent charge and achieves the same abatement at the same price. The difference is that with an effluent charge the control authority specifies a price and lets the firms determine their effluent quantity, whereas under a pollution rights scheme the authority specifies the total quantity and the firms determine the value of the right. With perfect information either plan could be used to achieve identical results.

The financial results for the firms should also be identical to those under an effluent charge. Marginal abatement costs would be equated, and each firm would pay a total abatement cost equal to the area under its abatement curve to the left of the intersection with the market price line. In addition, each firm must pay for the rights it purchased, so its outlays would include an amount equal to the expenditure on the effluent charge. And just as there is a possibility for a free base amount under an effluent charge to reduce the financial impact, so the control authority could offer a free allocation of rights to each firm under a pollution rights scheme that would reduce the financial burden there.

COMPARISON

Now that the three categories of pollution policies have been presented we can briefly summarize their relative merits. The first criterion, and the most difficult to evaluate, is social efficiency: how near the policies bring ambient environmental quality to an optimum level. With perfect information about pollution control costs and benefits, one can specify the optimal ambient quality. With this information and the assumption that ambient concentrations are proportional to emissions it would be easy to specify the total number of pollution rights necessary to achieve that ambient quality. It would be equally easy to determine an effluent charge that would result in the same total rate of emission. Finally, one could also fix an emission standard that would result in approximately the same net emissions. Note that because a uniform effluent standard does not minimize costs of control social welfare will be somewhat lower here than in the other two cases. While all policies can achieve the same environmental quality, their income effects differ, so that they will have somewhat different allocative properties.

In fact, of course, we rarely have perfect information about costs and usually have poor information about benefits. Under imperfect information the question is to find the program that comes closest to a desirable outcome. This depends upon the expected shape of the benefit and cost curves. Suppose, for example, that marginal pollution control costs are low and relatively constant over a wide range of control efficiencies. Assume further that at some point the damage from pollution rises sharply, perhaps because a physiological threshold has been exceeded. In such a case one could easily decide the desired ambient quality, just below the threshold, and variations in control costs would be modest. Here the specification of emission standards or emission rights can ensure that the threshold will not be exceeded, without risking high pollution control costs.

Suppose on the other hand that the costs of control are initially high and rise sharply as the degree of abatement is increased. Suppose further that the benefits of abatement are relatively constant with no serious threshold problems. It would now be relatively easy to specify a desired marginal abatement cost that approximated the marginal benefits and to allow the degree of control to adjust to equate the abatement costs and the charge. In this case, an effluent charge dominates over standards or rights that might inadvertently force polluters into the very high cost portion of the cost curve.

Where the benefits and costs are uncertain and the shape of their curves is not distinctive, as in the above cases, it is difficult to choose between policies. The emission rights scheme can begin with a total number of rights equal to current emissions and gradually reduce them in a predictable way by slowly withdrawing rights, or a low effluent charge could be instituted and gradually increased.

One important difference between the policies is their behaviour over time. Suppose that a legislative body fixes legislation now, not returning to the problem for ten or twenty years. If emission standards are used, economic and population growth will lead to gradually increased emissions as more and more polluters discharge their allowed emissions. A fixed effluent charge would also tend to allow more and more pollution with economic and population growth or inflation if technological progress did not occur. But we can ordinarily expect better and less expensive pollution controls over time; with an effluent charge these would tend to reduce total emissions. It is impossible to say a priori whether the growth in population and output would more or less than counterbalance the reduction in per unit emission due to technological change. In the case of emission rights, however, the long-run result is clear. Since the total emissions are specified they will remain constant; economic growth and population growth will not increase total emissions; technological progress and lower costs will not reduce emissions. In other words, when one can expect continuing neglect from the legislative authority there are clear differences between the policies.

With imperfect information it is difficult to choose between these policies on the ground of social efficiency alone. But the criterion of abatement efficiency is much easier to apply. We have noted than an effluent standard scheme applied uniformly will result in different marginal abatement costs among firms with different cost curves. The effluent charge and emission rights program, however, will result in equal marginal abatement costs for all polluters. It was demonstrated in the second chapter that total pollution control costs will be minimized by equating marginal abatement costs among polluters, assuming a perfectly mixed environment. Thus the effluent charge and the pollution rights scheme are equal and both superior to the effluent standard in abatement efficiency. Both can achieve a given total degree of pollution control at a lower abatement cost than can emission standards.

We have noted the importance of technological progress in reducing emission control costs over time. While an emission standards program provides incentives to achieve the currently legislated degree of control at ever lower costs, it is just like any other cost saving incentive to the polluter: it does not encourage the development of technology able to achieve higher degrees of control.

With effluent rights or effluent charges there is an incentive similar to that of a standard for reducing the costs of achieving current emission levels. But there is also an incentive to develop new means of further pollution reduction: the polluter benefits not only by abating more cheaply but also by abating further. Thus the effluent charge and pollution rights policies share an added technological incentive not present in emission standards. In the long run, abatement costs should be lower for these two policies because of greater technological change, and this factor may ultimately be far more important than even abatement efficiency.

Great debate has raged over the administrative costs of the alternative policies considered here. In the previous chapter we demonstrated that it should be less expensive to administer an effluent charge or emission rights policy than an effluent standards policy because average, not peak, emissions are being regulated. Thus the monitoring costs of the policy, a very large component of total administrative costs, should be lower for the two economic policies.

It is sometimes argued, however, that one can administer an effluent standard with minimal information, whereas one cannot impose an effluent charge unless one measures so precisely that the charge can be defended in court. The answer to this argument is that minimal monitoring is satisfactory for an effluent standard only when one is quite certain that most polluters are not close to the standard. If most polluters are much cleaner than necessary most of the time, only occasional monitoring is necessary to detect those close to the limit and isolate them for intensive monitoring to catch violations. Corresponding to this situation is the polluter who buys far more pollution rights than is necessary for his expected emissions. If you are entitled to pollute far more than you actually do, little monitoring will be necessary to ensure that you are nowhere near a violation. The only difference between these two situations is that with excess pollution rights the firm's expenditure is greater than if excess rights were not purchased, while with effluent standards only the clean-up cost is higher.

The criterion of equity has already been discussed in describing each policy. Pollution standards allow uniform emissions but widely varying marginal control costs. Rights and charges allow widely varying emissions but equal marginal abatement costs; they also allow widely varying total expenditures or average expenditures per unit emitted, depending upon the cost curve of the firm. The firm with inherently low pollution control costs has far lower expenses here. Since high cost firms may also be the old ones this may seem unfair. Another way to look at the difference is that the rights and charges policies require the polluter to pay for what he pollutes even after his clean-up, while the emission standard allows free use of the environment for the residual after controls are installed. In short the two economic schemes impose higher total costs on polluting industries than the emission standards. This is clearly efficient; whether it is equitable cannot be decided here.

NATIONAL VERSUS LOCAL POLICIES

We have seen that an environmental improvement program could set ambient air or water quality standards, emission standards, or an effluent charge. Even when the policy mechanism has been selected, there is still the problem of deciding what jurisdiction should impose the regulation, and over what area it should be uniform. We have seen in the second chapter that in some cases it is not desirable to have uniform standards even for a single river or river basin; yet some argue that environmental standards should be uniform across the entire nation.

An appropriate area of uniformity can be selected by returning to the criterion of balancing costs and benefits. In principle, emissions from each source should be controlled until the benefits from further abatement just equal the cost of that abatement. This implies a uniform effluent charge or environmental quality standard over any area in which the air or water can be regarded as well mixed. When the area becomes sufficiently large that ambient quality and therefore marginal benefits may vary significantly within the area, uniformity can no longer be defended on theoretical grounds. Thus there is no efficiency reason why two separate cities should have any similarity in their pollution control programs.

The discussion of costs and benefits noted that estimating the curves necessary to specify optimal conditions is difficult, if not impossible. Some general rules on the relationship of environmental policies between two areas or cities that differ in specific and well defined ways would therefore be useful. For example, it is more efficient for large cities to be dirtier or cleaner than small cities? If a city has particularly good ventilation does this mean that the allowable emission rate should be higher?

Peltzman and Tideman (1972) demonstrated that local setting of pollution charges would be more efficient in both the long run and the short run than uniform national changes, contrary to an earlier conclusion by Stein (1971). They argued that efficiency requires marginal benefits of abatement in any area to equal marginal costs of abatement in that area, and that both benefits and costs will tend to rise with increasing population and pollution-generating density, although not necessarily at the same rate. While the optimal pollution level might be similar in sparsely and densely populated cities, the optimal effluent charge would certainly be higher in the densely populated area than in the less populated one.

Useful results can be obtained by extending the Peltzman and Tideman analysis to cover the independent variations of population density P_i, pollution source density V_i, ventilation rate $1/K_i$, and initial air quality q_i^0. Various combinations of these four parameters for two cities have been explored. The relationship between the optimal air quality in the two cities q_1/q_2 and optimal effluent charges EC_1/EC_2 with linear benefits are presented in Table 14.

In the special situation of constant marginal benefits the effluent charges in both cities should be equal in only two cases: b and g. Where city 1 has better ventilation, less population, or both less pollution sources and less people its efficient effluent charge is less than that in city 2 by the exact proportion of those variables. These results confirm Peltzman and Tideman's conclusion that under these general assumptions the uniform national effluent charge cannot be efficient. Nor are ambient quality standards or emission standards efficient when uniform in all cities. With little information about the shape of the cost and benefit curves, the proper relationship between air pollution densities in two cities can sometimes be determined.

TABLE 14

Pollution control relationships for two cities

Initial conditions					Efficient pollution effluent density charge	
Case	P_1/P_2	V_1/V_2	K_1/K_2	$q_1{}^0/q_2{}^0$	q_1/q_2	EC_1/EC_2
a	1	1	a	a	$\geqq$	a
b	1	a	1	a	a	1
c	a	1	1	1	>1	a
d	1	a	β	$a\beta$	$\geqq a$	β
e	a	1	β	β	$>\beta$	$a\beta$
f	a	a	1	a	$>a$	a
g	a	a	$1/a$	1	1	1
h	1	a	$1/a$	1	<1	$1/a$

NOTE: P is population, V the number of sources, K the inverse of ventilation, q the pollution density, and EC the effluent charge. $0 < a < 1$; $0 < \beta < 1$

When city 1 has less population and fewer sources, but worse ventilation (case g), its efficient air quality is identical to city 2. When city 1 has fewer sources, and worse ventilation but the *same* population (case h), its efficient air quality is cleaner than city 2. And when the only difference is that city 1 has fewer sources (case b), or less population (case c) it should have cleaner air. Apparently, therefore, standards or charges set at the regional or local level are superior to national strictures. If a uniform national policy is inevitable, it should specify uniform environmental quality rather than uniform charges.

All this analysis has assumed that peoples' tastes for pollution are the same in all cities. If, in equilibrium, people have already voted with their feet, residents of dirty areas may be less sensitive to pollution than residents of more fortunate localities. This would tend to raise benefits in initially cleaner areas, increasing the efficient effluent charge there and lowering the efficient ambient pollution density. In such cases uniform standards are not clearly superior to uniform effluent charges. But again, local decision-making would lead to the proper solution while a uniform national policy would not – assuming, of course, that local governments accurately reflect the preferences of their constituency for such public goods as a clean environment. It is often argued that local government may reflect the wishes of concentrated interests (such as large industries) rather more faithfully than the dispersed wishes of individual voters. To the extent that this is true it would weigh against local setting of environmental policies, as long as higher government levels were more representative.

It should not be surprising that uniform quality standards or even uniform effluent charges are not efficient. Johnson (1967) demonstrated that even in a river a single effluent charge was not the least-cost means of achieving uniform ambient quality; the efficient solution was an effluent charge varying from one zone of the river to another. Two cities, which are less closely related than two stretches of the same river, should not need identical policies.

Dales (1968) makes the somewhat different argument that diversity itself is valuable. While it may be inevitable that cities are dirty because of industrial and individual sources of pollution, it may become more important to have clean areas to which city dwellers can retreat on weekends and holidays; but since these areas frequently have a very small permanent population, an empirical benefit measure, unless carefully estimated, would tend to be low for those areas, allowing high pollution levels. A uniform policy would tend to eliminate such pollution-free havens, while purely local decision-making might leave many remote areas even dirtier than urban areas, on a simple cost-benefit calculation. A true social accounting, Dales argues, would show greater benefits for these recreational areas and demand that they be maintained in a much cleaner state than urban areas.

It has been argued that uniform emission standards will eliminate incentives for industry to close plants because of pollution controls in one area (Bird and Waverman, 1972). This argument is certainly correct in assuming that different emission standards would lead to different marginal production costs in various areas and thus provide incentives for firms to move where the standards were more lenient and costs lower. The error is in assuming that this consequence is undesirable. If damages from emissions are much less in one area than in another, society is better off if heavily polluting industries locate in the former rather than in the latter. Their emissions will cause less social harm here. The migration of industries having high abatement costs from strict or high benefit areas to lenient or low benefit areas will improve social welfare and should be regarded not as a disaster but as a blessing.

The problem arises during the transition. If policies are instituted suddenly and rapid migrations take place there may be significant economic dislocations. The effect of these will be worse in areas where a few firms dominate a small labour market, since labour tends to be much less mobile than capital. This problem can be largely mitigated, however, by reasonable timing of policies. If new standards or charges are reached by gradual annual increments over a period of five to ten years, sufficient time can be allowed for an orderly movement of the industries that find migration to be the most economical solution. In any event, claims of large scale shutdowns or migrations resulting from pollution regulations must be closely scrutinized. In some cases the stricter pollution controls are merely the last straw for a failing firm or industry. If a firm closes or moves because of these regulations, but would have done so two years later for other reasons, the impact of the regulations is not the closing or migration itself but the two-year advance of this event. In short, it is important to separate the real from the apparent effects of these regulations.

ROLE OF ENVIRONMENTAL QUALITY STANDARDS

It has been argued that efficient pollution control requires that marginal benefits of control just equal the marginal cost, a point that can be reached by setting emission charges, emission standards, or ambient air or water quality standards. In practice, a common technique has been to establish a set of air and water quality standards or goals and adopt local emission control policies to achieve those ambient standards. The previous discussion suggests that uniform ambient quality standards are not an efficient way to determine ambient quality for all regions of the country. This approach is unable to equate marginal costs and benefits in widely differing areas; its primary attractions are simplicity and apparent equity, since all areas are in one sense treated alike. But the equity is of course only apparent since one could imagine a uniform effluent charge or a uniform emission standard that treats polluters 'equally' in some sense but leads to unequal environmental quality.

The uniform ambient standard has other problems. It requires further controls for any area that does not meet the standard and no more control for those that do, regardless of cost. The implications are that no benefits accrue from pollution control when quality is better than the standard and that benefits are infinite for areas above the standard. In short, the marginal benefit function instead of being a horizontal line or an upward sloping curve, as suggested by the data in most cases, looks like a step function: zero up to the standard and very large beyond that point. Since it is rare to have physiological thresholds below which there is no health effect and above which everyone is killed, this approach is prima facie unreasonable; it may be a close approximation only in some cases of water pollution where all damage relates to fish and a large proportion of a species may be killed by a small change in water quality. It is not a good description of many pollution problems.

But a policy with little to recommend it on theoretical grounds has not been so popular merely out of perversity. Baumol and Oates (1971) favour environmental quality standards combined with a pricing system to achieve these standards. They admit that the environmental quality standard will probably be set somewhat arbitrarily. In most cases pollution control benefits are difficult if not impossible to estimate, so that the ideal determination of an effluent charge and a standard is usually not possible. Thus, while the arbitrary specification of a standard may not be optimal, there may be no better practicable alternative. Furthermore, we are accustomed to determining qualities of public goods to be produced in many other fields such as police and fire protection and education; in deciding how many firemen or fire stations to have we do not worry greatly that we cannot estimate the marginal benefit of one more fireman or station. Since environmental quality is at least a physical quantity that most people can comprehend it may be more reasonable to set arbitrary ambient standards than to set emission standards or emission charges which most people could not in any way relate to the visible world around them.

It must be remembered that environmental quality standards are objectives, not enforceable laws. The ambient pollution density depends upon the emissions of all polluters in the area. If this density exceeds the environmental quality standard, it is usually impossible to decide which polluter has caused the excess; the combined emissions of many polluters have pushed the total beyond the prescribed limit. Penalties cannot reasonably be imposed on individual firms for causing the ambient standards to be exceeded. Rather, the ambient standard provides a yardstick against which to measure the success of emission charges or emission standards programs, and since the latter are applied directly to the polluter they can be enforced.

A partial exception occurs when the allowable emission rate or the emission charge is dependent upon ambient quality. When the ambient pollution density exceeds the ambient standard, individual emission standards may be tightened, or emission charges might automatically be increased. This has been proposed for water pollution control, where substantial damages may result from failing to meet an ambient quality level during predictable low-flow periods. Still, the ambient standard is only a mechanism for triggering individual emission standards or charges; it is not the final enforcement mechanism.

TIMING PROBLEMS

Pollution control is generally achieved by a combination of pollution abatement equipment, operating and maintenance changes, and some modification of the underlying production process. Changes in operating and maintenance procedures may be made quite rapidly if the desired change is well understood. The installation of pollution control equipment, on the other hand, may take a year or two for some firms, or even longer for others whose task is large. If an entire industry is required to install equipment simultaneously, it may take many years before suppliers of control equipment can satisfy all firms. In extreme cases the best way to control emissions is by switching to an entirely new production process, building new plants incorporating the new process and closing existing plants. Here the cost of control will be quite high unless sufficient time is given for old plants to approach the end of their normal economic life. Otherwise their productive capacity must be rendered valueless.

The magnitude of the capital investments required and the possible obsolescence of existing equipment render the timing of emission controls an important element in the cost of a control program. Designing a program so that the ultimate standards are reached after five or ten years may often result in far lower total costs than if the same results are required in one or two years. The cost savings from a gradual approach must be balanced against the increased emissions that it would allow. In the common case, where the cost per pound of pollution abated rises with increasing speed of abatement, the cost savings of a gradual program may be greater than the increased pollution damage.

One way to approximate this result is to require that new plants or equipment immediately incorporate the desired technology, meet the appropriate standard, or pay the applicable effluent charge, while old plants are faced with a more lenient requirement. One could specify that existing plants need not meet the same requirements as new ones until some considerable period of time had passed, to allow their conversion or closing in an orderly manner. This would reduce the dislocation costs of rapid imposition of controls, yet require that new investment incorporate the degree of control that has been identified as optimal for the future.

Another reason for careful consideration of timing is technological progress. Where emission controls are applied to a source or industry for the first time, it may be anticipated that the initial control strategies will be primitive and costly. As experience is gathered, however, new and better methods of pollution control are invariably found. Several years of intensive research and development may produce systems that are much more effective and much less costly than those initially available; sometimes costs drop by 50 to 75 per cent over a few years. It is therefore important to devise regulatory strategies to encourage the maximum technological progress, without incurring excessive costs in the interim.

Another argument for a gradual approach to effluent charges or emission standards is that we rarely know precisely what environmental quality is desired or would result from a given policy. It may be apparent that current environmental quality is inadequate, but not how much environmental quality would be best. If a gradual program of pollution reduction is undertaken, experience can be gained in the costs of abatement and the resulting environmental quality. This will allow the program to establish an environmental quality level and effluent charge or emission standard that provides a good balance between costs and benefits, without overshooting and incurring high costs or undershooting and requiring revision of the standards.

All these arguments for a gradual approach, of course, are equally arguments in favour of effluent charges rather than standards. An emission standard requires a specific degree of abatement upon a specific date; an effluent charge simply imposes a cost on high levels of emission. If an industry finds that it is expensive to clean up in a hurry, it can pay the effluent charge until the abatement can be achieved more economically. A regulatory agency relying on effluent charges need not second-guess the industry on the appropriate abatement schedule; it need only establish an effluent charge at a level that will not be punitive and an orderly timing of emission control should result.

Thus the general ignorance about future (and even present) costs and benefits gives a great advantage to gradual policies that can incorporate information gathered in the early stages to modify the policy.

SUMMARY

The considerations involved in choosing an emission control policy are so numerous and diverse that no simple prescription can cover all cases. When measurement and enforcement problems are considered it is difficult even to catalogue, much less to analyse, the performance of various alternative policies. This summary therefore, only suggests a general set of conclusions: it is not a short cut to legislative drafting.

If the environmental problem under consideration is not serious and little actual reduction in the emission rate is desired, emission standards may be the dominant policy. Since they have been the primary form of regulation for decades, many legal examples are available to choose from. Since no action need be taken against the polluter unless a violation of the standard is observed, measurement costs can be as low as desired. If the budget will allow only surveillance in response to complaints about pollution problems, and this method of monitoring is undertaken, there will be little reduction in emissions, but at least monitoring and enforcement costs will be small.

But if the pollution problem is a serious one, and substantial reductions in emission rates are desired, the emission standard loses much of its attractiveness. Where substantial and expensive pollution control programs must be undertaken a large-scale monitoring program will undoubtedly be necessary regardless of the policy instrument used. In fact an emission standard would likely require more measurement than an emission charge or emission rights program. Since there is no measurement cost penalty here the efficiency advantages of the two market solutions suggest that they dominate the standard. They have the further advantage of promoting technological progress in the most efficient manner. Their primary disadvantage is that they impose costs on polluters beyond expenditures for pollution control equipment; as indicated above this may cause political problems, but from an economic point of view it is undoubtedly desirable.

The choice between an effluent charge program and an effluent rights program should depend upon the expected nature of the cost and benefit curves and the behaviour of pollution sources over time. If the desired environmental quality can be specified with some certainty and the cost of achieving that standard is not anticipated to be too high, an effluent rights scheme would be in order. It provides reasonable certainty about the resulting environmental quality, and with well behaved cost functions does not risk inordinate control costs. On the other hand, if the benefits of pollution control do not vary significantly with the degree of control and costs are variable or highly uncertain, an effluent charge may be in order. A charge in this case leaves the expected degree of control uncertain but places a clear upper limit on total costs imposed on polluters. In the many cases not covered by these specific situations, some judgment must be exercised on the relative desirability of uncertain environmental quality and uncertain control costs.

The policy need not always apply at the point of emission. Where the primary determinant of the emission rate is the capital equipment and where there are enough sources to make frequent monitoring expensive the policy may be applied at the time of sale of the equipment. For example, automobiles may be regulated by limiting emission rates from new cars without regulations on maintenance of used cars. This regulation at the point of sale would probably be recommended for most consumer goods. An effluent standard could be applied, as in the case of automobiles, or an effluent charge could be levied. This would be in a form of a 'potential pollution' charge proportional to the expected emissions of the equipment over its economic life (Dewees, 1974).

There seems little economic reason for nationally uniform pollution control policies. If the objective is to equate benefits and costs of pollution control, the best way is on a region, airshed, or watershed basis. Nationwide standards or charges would be appropriate only for mobile sources and for pollution so widely dispersed that benefits are equal in all areas. Alternatively, one might set quite a lenient national standard or charge, intending it to be but a first step towards more complete local control. The national program would be designed to be appropriate for the least polluted areas, assuming that more severely polluted areas could add further charges or more stringent standards.

RESEARCH RECOMMENDATIONS

It should be clear from the discussion above that legislation for controlling specific pollution problems must generally be preceded by research to determine the proper degree of control and the best policy instrument to achieve it. In other chapters we have suggested areas in which additional research might be particularly useful for environmental policy decisions. The following will briefly summarize these recommendations.

Perhaps the most important area to be investigated is the cost and effectiveness of alternative monitoring programs. Much of the debate over the relative merits of alternative policies seems to turn on the question of measurement or monitoring costs, yet there are few empirical studies to support any of the competing positions. Theoretical studies of the measurement needs of alternative policies should be undertaken. Empirical studies should be launched to determine the cost of alternative monitoring procedures and the precision of discharge rate estimates that can be made from alternative monitoring techniques. The past experience of various jurisdictions could be evaluated and combined with technical-economic studies to assess alternative monitoring systems not already implemented.

A more traditional area of research is the further investigation of pollution control cost functions for industries likely to be regulated in the near future. The kinds of cost relationships already available for new installations of sewage treatment facilities or electrostatic precipitators could be developed for a variety of other control techniques and emission sources. This research should be directly related to future policy needs since the area of exploration is so vast that it could consume any conceivable research budget. If limited amounts are to be spent they must be well directed.

It is clear that in many cases technological progress in pollution control is the most important determinant of control costs at any time. Especially in areas where controls have not previously been applied we can anticipate that control costs will drop dramatically if sufficient pressure is applied so that technological research and development is undertaken. It would be of tremendous value to have better information about the rate of change of control costs as a function of the type of policy applied and the degree of stringency required. A number of economic studies might be undertaken to explore this relationship between the technological progress in pollution control and a variety of explanatory variables. Already there should be sufficient data to allow reasonably reliable empirical results.

Some effort should undoubtedly be placed on examination of the benefits of pollution control. The methodological and data problems in estimating benefits, however, suggest that it will not be possible to develop precise quantitative estimates within a few years. Furthermore, an enormous amount of research is currently under way in the United States, the results of which might be adapted to the Ontario situation. This suggests two fruitful directions to pursue. One is to collect existing studies of pollution damages from other countries, principally the United States, and develop methodologies for adapting these results to Ontario. This would maximize the usefulness of existing studies and produce significant results at reasonably low cost. The second would be to develop relationships between the desired environmental quality in different regions within the province. Even if the dollar magnitude of benefits for controlling some pollutant cannot be estimated, it may be possible to indicate the relative level of benefits in different areas. This would be useful for formulating policies suited to local conditions rather than arbitrarily uniform ones.

Finally, some research can be based upon the fact that environmental decisions are often made with little information and generate further cost and benefit data as the control program progresses. In many cases the best policy is to embark upon a modest pollution control program and monitor the costs of achieving that program and the changes in various benefit indexes that result. Research could be undertaken to design monitoring and surveillance programs that would best utilize the information resulting from pollution control programs, allowing what is learned in the first few years of a program to be incorporated in subsequent modifications. Because such feedback policies have not been widely investigated in the past, it is important to undertake research now to determine how such programs might operate.

7
Selected case studies

This chapter presents case studies of three current pollution problems in Ontario. The cases selected are quite different from one another, but each has presented difficulty in finding an appropriate solution. More unusual cases were selected because the common cases of particulate emission or organic effluent have been discussed in sufficient detail that their analysis should be clear. In general, a final solution to each problem is not selected, although several are suggested, because an ultimate decision would require information not currently available or value judgments that ought to be made by the public or their representatives, not by an analyst.

LEAD EMISSIONS IN METROPOLITAN TORONTO

Two apparent sources of lead have recently been the subject of much public debate in Toronto. These are the Canada Metal plant on Eastern Avenue and Toronto Refiners and Smelters Ltd, on Bathurst Street. Both plants operate secondary lead smelters in areas of mixed residential and industrial properties. Canada Metal, which has been in operation since 1925, produces lead, lead alloys, and lead oxide by the Barton oxide process. A wide range of copper, zinc, and lead alloys are also produced at Roto Cast Ltd, an affiliate of Canada Metal located at the same plant. Toronto Refiners and Smelters has been recovering lead from lead-bearing scrap, such as used storage batteries, for twenty-five years. The recovery process includes transportation, crushing, smelting, and refining, and each stage emits lead.

Incidence of lead pollution

1 / Toronto Refiners and Smelters Ltd

The back yards of many houses in this area share a common property line with the smelting plant. It has been alleged that the Toronto Refiners and Smelters Ltd is a source of 'excessive lead contamination' up to distances of five hundred feet from the property line (Ontario, 1973b, 7) and that the occupants of these houses live in an environment of above-normal lead concentrations.

Controls presently being used at this plant include baghouses to collect particles from the in-plant process, pavement of heavily travelled areas, and washing the wheels of outgoing trucks. The abatement of lead emissions from the flue gas with baghouses is currently adequate, hence the problem emissions probably result from inadequacies in the other abatement measures. The evidence suggests that high suspended lead levels exist only in areas very close to the plant. This can be explained largely by fugitive dust emissions from battery crushing operations and materials handling (Ontario, 1973a). Since the particulates emitted from these operations are rather large they stay airborne only for short periods.

One study concluded that lead is taken into the body mainly by ingestion rather than by inhalation (ibid.); it seems therefore that air quality indicies would tend to understate the area's health problem. The lead content of the soil is probably a more relevant indicator of the magnitude of the problem: soil lead contents near the plant are ten to one hundred times those a few blocks away (see Figure 16). Lead content in park soils within a two-mile radius of the centre city averages about 710 μg/gm (Air Pollution Working Group, 1974b, 11). It has also been suggested that significant contributions to existing lead levels, above those from automotive and other industrial sources, can be attributed to the smelter (Ontario, 1973b).

2 / Canada Metal Ltd

There are houses located within one hundred feet of the Canada Metal property line. As with the Toronto Refiners and Smelters, ore handling and dust generating activities within the plant area are the important source of emissions (Air Pollution Working Group, 1974a, 12). Soil lead concentrations in the adjacent area are ten to fifty times the levels found several blocks away (see Figure 17). Control practices currently used by this firm include baghouses on various emission sources, pavement of 60 per cent of the heavily travelled areas, and washing the wheels of outgoing trucks. The installation of a new baghouse and pavement of the remaining heavily travelled areas remain to be completed, in fulfilment of a control order issued by the Ontario Department of the Environment on 23 March 1973 (Ontario, 1973b).

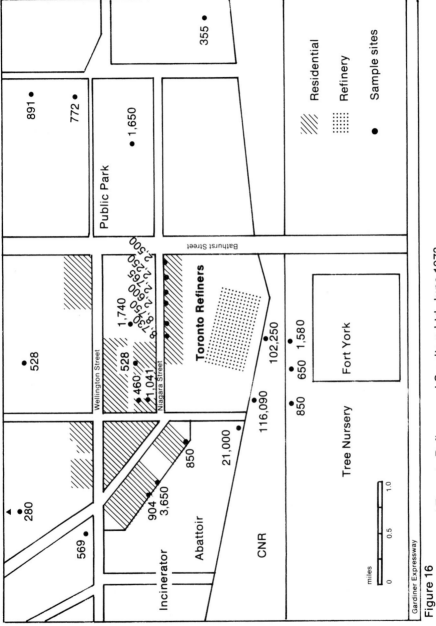

Figure 16
Lead in soil around Toronto Refiners and Smelters Ltd, June 1973
(in µg/g. From Air Pollution Working Group, 1974b)

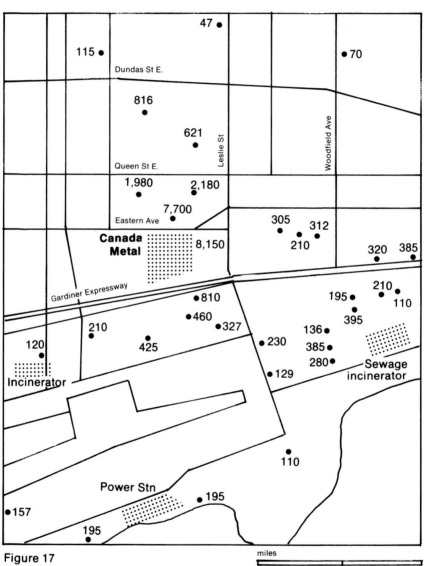

Figure 17
Lead in soil around Canada Metal Ltd
(in μg/g. From Air Pollution Working Group, 1974a)

The interim report of the provincial authorities (ibid.) came to the following conclusions about Canada Metal: that Canada Metal and Roto Cast Ltd were sources of undesirable lead contamination up to fifteen hundred feet from the plant, and that available evidence discounted incinerators and vehicular traffic as significant contributors to lead levels found close to the plant.

Because emissions from both Canada Metal and Toronto Refiners and Smelters are largely a result of ore handling and dust generating activities, no standard cost figures for abatement are available.

Damages from lead pollution

Emissions from these smelters have allegedly caused a significant elevation of blood lead levels in the population surrounding the plants. Table 15 shows the

TABLE 15

Percentage distribution of lead in blood in communities near smelters and a control area

Blood lead level (ugs/100 mls)	Control area (Euclid/Bloor)		Toronto Refiners		Canada Metal	
	Total sample	Children	Total sample	Children	Total sample	Children
0- 9	9	10	0	0	1	0
10-19	64	70	6.5	0	25	13
20-29	22	20	25	24	46	42
30-39	5	0	41	47	21	23
40-49	0	0	18.5	18	5	16
50-59	0	0	9	11	1	3
60+	0	0	0	0	0.5	3
Number in sample	45	12	32	17	698	31
Mean	17	18	33	35	n.a.	31

NOTE: Results are expressed as percentages of the sample total. Canada Metals total sample percentages derived from data supplied by the Toronto medical officer of health.
SOURCE: Air Pollution Working Group (1974b)

results of blood samples taken both from smelter neighbourhoods and from a control neighbourhood located far from any significant source of lead pollution. A normal adult has a blood lead level of 15 to 40 μg/100 ml. Although no lead is required by the body, levels in this range do not produce adverse symptoms. Lead levels greater than 60 μg/100 ml are considered critical because of the impairment of aminolevulinic acid dehydrase (ALAD), an enzyme necessary for the synthesis of hæmoglobin (Bini, 1973, 133). There is no agreement, however, about whether a moderate amount of ALAD impairment is really harmful

(Canadian Lead Industries Association, 1974; Labour Council of Metropolitan Toronto et al., 1974), but blood levels greater than 80 $\mu g/100$ ml are dangerous for an adult (Bini, 1973, 133). At this level lead intoxication may occur, manifesting itself through dysfunction of the alimentary tract and less often through neuromuscular syndrome, lead encephalopathy, and cerebrovascular catastrophe (Labour Council of Metropolitan Toronto et al., 1974).

Children appear to be more susceptible than adults to lead poisoning; by eating non-food substances they increase the amount of lead they ingest and there is some evidence that they absorb and retain a greater percentage of ingested lead (ibid.). And as might be expected their tolerance is lower than adults': children with as low as 20 $\mu g/100$ ml blood level have shown ALAD interference, and a level of 40 $\mu g/100$ ml is considered critical (ibid.). Children exhibiting symptoms of lead intoxication have been found to have blood-lead levels in the range of 60 to 100 $\mu g/100$ ml (Bini, 1973).

The most important damage from lead pollution in these cases appears to be the alleged impairment of the surrounding population's health, a kind of damage it is difficult to place a value on. First, there is no agreement on the harm caused by elevated blood lead levels that may cause ALAD inhibition but not lead intoxication. Substantial damage may be caused by low blood lead levels sustained over a long period; on the other hand the only damage may be an increased probability that further exposure will result in clinical symptoms. Even when intoxication is present its earlier symptoms may easily be confused with those of other diseases, so that accurate data on the portion of the population suffering clinical symptoms is difficult to obtain.

The final problem in quantifying the health damage stems from the fact that primarily children are affected by the lead concentrations present in Toronto. The value of wages lost during absence from work, the economic cost of a disease, is not an applicable measure for calculating health damages to children. Nevertheless, it is apparent that families and children themselves do place a value on the children's health and substantial expenditures are made to protect and maintain it; possibly only the families themselves can place an accurate value on these losses.

Even if one could obtain a schedule of the marginal health benefits for the existing population, this schedule might be based on a non-optimal population in the area. If, for instance, the lead emissions were not detected in the past, or their harmful effects were not understood, more houses could have been constructed and inhabited near the plants than would have been the case if accurate information about the pollution and its effects were available. Because houses are a durable investment, a supraoptimal population would persist long after the danger became known. On the other hand, if more than the optimal amount of emissions has been allowed and its harm suspected, demand for housing in the area will have been depressed and there will be a smaller population than in the presence of properly controlled emissions. Conversely, although less likely, if current regulations are too strict there may be too many persons in the area, and the correct solution would involve less population in the immediate area and less strict regulation. In order to avoid constant adjustment of policies as population enters and leaves the neighbourhood, the benefit function must be defined on the basis of the optimum population level (Baumol, 1972, 314-15). This compounds the problem of measuring abatement benefits since it necessitates the inclusion in our calculations of a relationship between the emission level and the population.

Some suggested solutions to this problem

1 / Bargaining
Many of the difficulties in measuring the benefits of abatement could be circumvented if negotiation between the companies and the residents were possible and if the harmful effects of the pollution were well understood by those residents. Where, as in these cases, the affected area is well defined and the residents have already organized local associations to deal with the issue, one might expect the type of negotiation suggested by Coase (1960) and described in our second chapter. But it has not taken place here, in part because of the absence of a clearly defined property right. The smelters believe that they have a right to emit lead into the air and that the political and judicial authorities may sustain this right. Similarly, the residents believe that they have a right to limit the amount of lead falling on their land and that this may be upheld: Once a property right is assigned, bargaining may take place, resulting either in payment of compensation by the firm to the residents or payment for reduced emissions by the residents to the firm. In this solution all parties would be at least as well off as before bargaining (but after imposition of the property right) and some better off.

   In Figure 18 ABE_0 is the marginal cost of abatement or the marginal net gain to the polluter from each unit of emissions, OBC is the marginal damages to residents, and OE_0 the current and OE_1 the optimal level of emissions. Bargaining under the conditions depicted would begin from point O if the residents controlled the property right or from point E_0 if the firm controlled the property right; in either case bargaining would reduce emissions to point E_1. In the first case the firm would pay more than OE_1B but less than OE_1BA, the movement from O to E_1 being such that neither party is made worse off and at

Figure 18
Marginal costs and benefits of smelter emission reductions

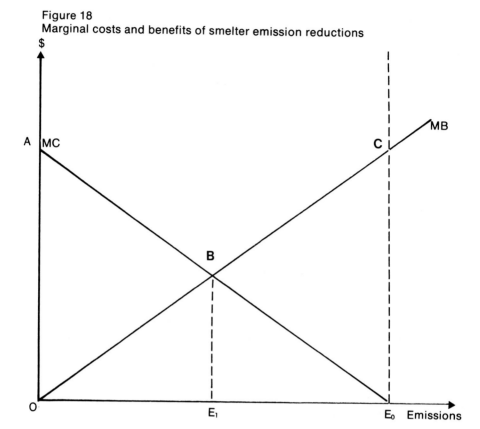

least one party is made better off.[1] If the firm owned the right, the residents
would pay more than control costs E_0E_1B, but less than benefits E_0E_1BC.[2]

1 At the starting point O, the firm will spend OAE_0 on abatement and the residents will
  benefit to the extent OCE_0 relative to a position of uncontrolled emission. Bargaining
  would lead to a situation in which the firm would emit OE_1. The tenants would accept
  this result in exchange for an amount greater than OBE_1. The maximum bribe the firm
  will offer is $OABE_1$. If the residents receive this maximum bribe they gain OBA over
  the benefits they were achieving with zero emissions; the firm meanwhile would be no
  better or worse off.
2 Because different property right assignments will have different, and perhaps substantial,
  income effects, the final equilibrium emissions level may be different in the two cases.
  It is only by assuming no income effect that it is possible to simplify the problem to
  this extent.

A simple regulatory solution, however, will not result in such a mutually beneficial movement from the initial point. Starting from point E_0, a regulatory solution requiring abatement by the firm will make the firm worse off and the residents better off. In addition, the government, not knowing the relevant damage schedule, must either arbitrarily choose a point between the extremes O and E_0 or accede to the demands of one or the other party. It is unlikely in this case that such a solution will be Pareto optimal unless the regulatory agency has cost and benefit information at least as good as that of the parties themselves. Hence, by this criterion bargaining is the superior solution.

Bargaining may cause the smelter to go out of business or to buy all the residential property, and this indeed may be optimal. We reviewed in the third chapter an actual case in Polk County, Florida, where fertilizer plants were given the choice of abating their emissions or buying affected lands (Crocker, 1969); they found it cheaper to buy cattle lands than to abate, but this was not the case for citrus fruit lands. Since the firms were not given the choice of partially abating and compensating the growers for the injuries still incurred, the final outcome cannot be assumed to be optimal. Nevertheless, the solution of limited option bargaining was superior to the government emission standard later established because the individuals involved could recognize that certain lands were more productive as dumping grounds for waste fluorides than in any alternative use. A bargaining approach to the lead problems in Toronto could lead to the same type of evaluation of the alternatives by the parties involved.

2 / Barriers to bargaining

A negotiated solution can raise several problems not seriously examined by Coase. First, the original property right assignment will result in a windfall gain either to the residents or to the companies. This will be an irreversible gain or loss to the parties since any payments to be made under a negotiated settlement will be immediately discounted into the price of land and the business that subsequent entrants must pay. The assignment of the property right requires some subjective value judgement since little can be said about it on efficiency grounds; it is basically a question of equity which the relevant representative authorities must decide. Therefore, careful consideration must be given to the social desirability of such decisions.

Secondly, the proper incentives to bargain must be present. This requires that the property right be clearly established and easily enforced by the party entitled to it. There may also be some question about the ability of residents or residents' representatives to bargain effectively. If few experts can agree about the effects of lead emissions, residents cannot be expected to know their relevant damage function. If residents' groups have less information on the damages of lead emissions than do certain government authorities bargaining would be a hollow exercise.

Finally, the residents must be prepared to abide by the settlement negotiated by their associations. Giving these associations a degree of authority they have not previously held would be particularly important if the property rights were vested in the companies rather than in the residents and the associations were negotiating payments *by* the residents rather than *to* them. Reorganizing these bodies on more formal and representative lines would be necessary in either case.

3 / An imposed solution

While a negotiated solution seems best in a case with a single polluter, a small number of pollutees, and a clearly defined dispersion path and causal relationship, any of these problems might render negotiation impracticable. The only recourse then would be for the government to set emission standards or charges, which would require estimate of marginal damages and marginal abatement costs at various levels of emissions from the lead plant.

To derive the damage-emission function the relationship between damages and ambient air quality must first be estimated. Then, with the aid of a dispersion model, the effect of changing emissions on ambient air and soil concentrations near the emitter can be determined. By combining these two relationships one could describe the incremental damage caused by various levels of emissions.

One technique of deriving the relationship between ambient air quality and damages would be to determine the value of various types of damage caused at different levels of lead pollution. A major component of such a study would be health costs; the medication and treatment costs for lead poisoning could be calculated as described in our third chapter, but the costs of subclinical effects or loss of future productive capacity of currently affected children cannot easily be determined. An alternative approach would be a property-value study similar to those done by Zerbe, Ridker and Henning, or Anderson and Crocker, which were discussed in the second section of that chapter.

Unless the health damages are accurately perceived by the residents the property value study cannot adequately capture these damages. Thus uncertainty about the effects of the pollution may be as much a barrier to sensible government intervention as to a negotiated solution.

Since lead emission problems arise because of ore handling and dust generating activities, abatement alternatives include reductions in output, more careful handling of materials, paving of heavily travelled areas, roofed enclosures for scrap lead piles, and so on. The level of abatement achieved by varying degrees of these alternatives and the costs involved with each could provide a least-cost schedule for achieving various levels of abatement. The second section of chapter 4 suggests a methodology for constructing such a schedule. With the engineering estimates necessary to provide the component costs this technique would yield the most cost-effective result for any given degree of abatement.

A major difficulty in enforcing any solution to the smelter problem is measuring the emission rate. Since the trouble lies in fugitive dust emissions rather than stack emissions, accurate measurements from the Toronto lead smelters are probably not feasible. One solution would be to measure lead dust-fall at the smelter property line and attribute this to the smelter: since these concentrations are currently far above the other urban lead levels, other sources would not seriously interfere with such measurements, and since lead in the soil is the major health problem, dustfall measurements would be closely related to the purpose of the measurements. Ambient dustfall measurements would probably be used for any regulatory scheme adopted here.

It would not be surprising if no dollar value could be placed on health benefits, and only rough estimates of costs made for different control levels. In such a case, a pure effluent charge is not possible, and the regulatory body would probably have to decide either to insist that the dustfall be reduced to some arbitrary standard between current levels and those found elsewhere in the city or to purchase and evacuate the houses. Giving the companies the option to buy the houses would allow them to choose the least cost of these two alternatives. The dustfall standard could be enforced by an effluent charge for any excess over the standard great enough to ensure ultimate compliance. Least desirable would be government demands for specific abatement actions, since they would not allow the smelter to choose least-cost control techniques nor ensure any particular level of environmental quality unless the effectiveness of the procedures were known for certain.

In summary: the limited number of pollutees for each polluter, the clear causal relation between the polluters and ambient lead levels, and the historical persistence of this problem suggest a negotiated solution in the lead smelter cases. If information problems or unequal bargaining power (high transaction costs) render bargaining ineffective the next best alternative would be to set an ambient lead standard and require the smelters to meet the standard or buy the houses. The standard should be enforced by an effluent charge for any excess, designed to ensure ultimate compliance without undue financial strain. For any solution the difficult emissions monitoring problem could be surmounted by an ambient dustfall monitoring program.

SULPHUR OXIDE EMISSIONS IN THE SUDBURY AIR SHED

The two largest firms in the Sudbury area operating nickel mines and smelters are the International Nickel Company of Canada (INCO) and Falconbridge Nickel Mines Ltd. In 1970 INCO and Falconbridge supplied approximately 80 per cent of the non-Communist world's production of nickel, although not entirely from Sudbury. This represented a total output of nickel by INCO of 519 million pounds and by Falconbridge of 161 million pounds (Paehlke, 1973, 33). The majority of this output has been exported and represents a significant factor in Canada's balance on current accounts. Other metals produced by these companies include platinum, gold, iron, and copper, but nickel is by far the most important metal mined and smelted in the area. INCO's smelters are located at Copper Cliff, approximately five miles west of Sudbury;[3] Falconbridge's smelters are located approximately 10 miles northeast of town.

Sulphur dioxide emissions
Smelters in the Sudbury area emit more than two million tons of sulphur dioxide each year, compared to 3.5 million tons of sulphur dioxide emitted from ore smelters in the entire United States (Linzon, 1971, 81). Heavy metals are also emitted in several forms but are not analysed in this study.

Income per capita in Sudbury is the highest of any major city in Canada (Financial Post, 1973). Many factors could explain this phenomenon, including the level of pollution in Sudbury: perhaps wages must be elevated to induce a worker to remain in Sudbury and compensate him for damages suffered. Higher wages, however, would not fully internalize this externality. Sulphur dioxide remains airborne up to several days (Bangay, 1973, 38), so that areas outside Sudbury may be affected by smelter emissions depending on geographical position, wind speed and direction, and other meteorological conditions. In fact, ambient sulphur dioxide concentrations can persist at distances in excess of twenty miles.

As noted in the second chapter, sulphur dioxide can cause a variety of damages, summarized in Table 1. This chemical and the sulphuric acid mists it produces are responsible for damage to metals, building materials, paint, leather, paper, textiles, dyes, and ceramics.

Sulphur dioxide is also known to cause substantial damage to vegetation in and around Sudbury. In 1971, 1,950 square miles around Sudbury were exposed to at least one potentially injurious fumigation, 380 square miles to ten such incidents and 75 square miles to twenty (Erickson, 1973, 29). A potentially damaging sulphur dioxide fumigation is defined as a level exceeding 0.95 ppm for one hour; 0.55 ppm for two hours; 0.35 ppm for four hours; or 0.25 ppm for eight hours (ibid., 28). One study of the Sudbury smelter district, which examined the economic loss from chronic injury to vegetation caused by long-term

3 INCO also had a smelter located at Coniston, nine miles east of Sudbury, but it was closed in May 1972.

absorption of sulphur dioxide over a ten-year period, estimated that in an area of 720 square miles around Sudbury the loss to woodlot owners in total revenue from white pine alone was about $117,000 per annum.[4]

A number of studies discussed in the second section of chapter 3 show the effect of sulphur dioxide on health. Lave (1972), for instance, has shown that a reduction in the minimum level by 1 $\mu g/m^3$ (0.00035 ppm) will decrease the total mortality rate per ten thousand population by 0.85. Since the average level of sulphur dioxide in Sudbury itself is about 60 $\mu g/m^3$, compared to a mean value of 46.9 $\mu g/m^3$ for the area used in Lave's study, his results should be applicable there. The chemical has also been shown to affect morbidity from diseases as varied as lung cancer and the common cold.

Sulphur dioxide emissions from the Sudbury smelters can probably also be blamed for several severe cases of water pollution. Sixty miles southwest of Sudbury, in and around Killarney Provincial Park, thirty-three lakes are in critical condition and thirty-seven others endangered because of low pH levels; similar trends are also being observed northeast of Sudbury in the Lake Temagami region (Bangay, 1973, 38). These conditions have been attributed to Sudbury smelter emissions.

The problem
The situation currently existing in the Sudbury airshed is a classic example of an externality. The smelters have appropriated the use of the environment at no cost to themselves, whereas the cost to other members of society, including woodlot owners, tourists, and inhabitants of the airshed, in terms of foreclosed opportunities and actual damages is large.

Bargaining among the parties is a less reasonable solution to this problem than it was in the lead smelter cases because of the large number of pollutees and the greater problems of proof. With the lead smelters the primary pollution effects were within one or two blocks of the plants and could be clearly attributed to them because no other sources were nearby. In this case the gases travel great distances and damages are incurred over hundreds of square miles. Since it would be difficult to determine the proportion of damage to each resident or property owner attributable to a specific source because of varying meteorological conditions a negotiated solution is virtually ruled out.

Government action will therefore be necessary. It could involve an emission standard or an effluent charge designed to meet some ambient air quality goal.

4 Linzon, 1971, 86. Note that eastern white pine represents only about 7.6 per cent of the productive forest area in the 720-square-mile area considered (ibid.). The damage figure given, however overestimates the social loss because of factors discussed in the second section of chapter 3.

The choice between these two policies will depend in part upon the shape of the marginal cost and marginal benefit curves for abating smelter emissions of sulphur dioxide.

Benefits and costs of sulphur dioxide emission control

1 / Benefits of abatement
The marginal-benefit-of-abatement schedule represents the social value of marginal damages forgone at various levels of abatement. This section is concerned with deriving that schedule.

Sulphur dioxide damage can be divided into its effect on materials, on vegetation, and on health. Separate studies could be carried out on each and the results combined to derive the over-all relationship between damages and ambient air quality.

No study has yet determined the economic value of the material damages suffered from different levels of air pollution. The reason even well constructed studies show no significant relationship between sulphur dioxide levels and material damage is that the effects of pollution are small in comparison with those of other factors. With its high pollution levels Sudbury might therefore be an ideal place for a study of the kind done by Ridker (1967) relating the frequency of repainting or other maintenance with the ambient air quality.

The damage done to vegetation in the Sudbury area at various levels of air quality could be estimated with a property value study similar to that done by Crocker (1969) and discussed in the third chapter.

Such a study would try to explain the value of forest properties by a measure of ambient air quality, perhaps using both the frequency of harmful fumigations and the mean level of sulphur dioxide, in order to account for long-term mild exposures and frequent short-term severe exposures. Other variables that contribute to the valuation of this property should also be included. The price differential between lands similar except for their pollution levels would then be a measure of the present value of expected losses in both lumbering and recreational uses.[5] Similar studies could be conducted for agricultural land or any other category of property in order to determine the present value of expected future losses from sulphur dioxide. These property value studies would measure the damage perceived by buyers and sellers of land; if dollar values of the reduced agricultural or forest yield of the properties were available, they could substitute for the property values as a damage measure.

---

5 Including losses due to water pollution that kills fish and otherwise destroys the desirability of the water body for recreation.

Health costs of sulphur dioxide pollution were also discussed in the third chapter. Lave's (1972) figures enable us to estimate that a reduction of 1 $\mu g/m^3$ would save approximately seventeen lives per year, assuming a population in the Sudbury area of about 200,000. If we assume that these individuals have lost an average of five working years and take the average yearly income as about $8,000, the present value of the annual loss, in 1971 dollars, calculated with real rate of interest of 4 per cent, is approximately $580,767. This figure does not include losses due to premature disposal or any of the treatment costs, all of which must be included in a determination of total health costs.

Combining all these categories, material damages, vegetation damages, health damages, and fishing damages, will aid in determining an approximate figure for over-all damages at various levels of ambient air quality. This schedule can then be used to determine the incremental benefit-of-abatement schedule.

The shape of the marginal benefit schedule is just as important as its absolute magnitude. The evidence suggests that while most effects do not appear below some threshold concentration this threshold is different for each effect; as concentrations increase, more and more types of damage occur. This suggests a marginal benefit function that increases with concentration in an irregular fashion. Unless all thresholds coincide, or one is of paramount importance, it does not suggest a step in the benefit function which would imply that a single ambient quality standard was optimal. Instead, it appears that any reduction in emissions would be valuable and more so at higher ambient concentrations, though there may be some low concentration level below which further benefits are not perceptible.

2 / Costs of abatement

As was emphasized in chapter 4, all methods of abatement should be considered when determining the minimum cost of achieving a lower emission level. The alternatives open to the smelters in the Sudbury region include reducing output, changing processes, constructing high stacks, and tail-end controls. By determining the level of abatement achieved by, and the costs associated with, each of these alternatives it is possible to derive a least-cost schedule for the achievement of various levels of abatement. The programming algorithm necessary to achieve this result has been suggested in chapter 4.

Tail-end methods of abating sulphur dioxide (i.e. mechanical abatement methods) from smelter gases sometimes yield a waste by-product, such as limestone scrubbing, and sometimes a marketable by-product, such as the elemental sulphur recovery system used at Falconbridge. Techniques leaving waste by-products should include disposal among the abatement costs and, where appropriate, amenity costs of the type discussed in chapter 4. Similarly, processes leaving marketable by-products such as elemental sulphur or sulphuric acid should reduce estimated costs to reflect revenues generated. To evaluate properly abatement techniques involving the production of different marketable by-products, market studies reflecting future supply and demand conditions may be required; the price of sulphur, for instance, is sometimes very low.

A large tail-end abatement project was operated for two years at a Falconbridge facility. This installation was equivalent in size to that necessary for the removal of 90 per cent of the sulphur dioxide from the flue gas of a 2000 MW thermal power station burning 4 per cent sulphur fuel oil and produced five hundred tons per day of elemental sulphur (Hunter, 1973, 63). The advantages of this process over others involving the production of sulphuric acid are lower storage and shipping costs.

Such prototype projects lack the detailed information to suggest control costs for the smelter as a whole. Such a cost analysis requires data on the following: all emission sources in the smaller complex, details of the emissions from these sources, the abatement techniques available for each source, including changing input and output mix, and the problems involved in the various control techniques. Ignorance of these facts makes any attempt at estimating control costs for the Sudbury smelters extremely precarious. Consulting firm studies and cost estimates are probably necessary to determine an adequate solution to this problem.

The chief source of abatement currently used by INCO at Copper Cliff is a 1,250-foot stack, which cost $25 million to construct in 1972. This has changed the pattern of damages observed in the Sudbury region, in particular reducing sulphur dioxide concentrations and damage in the city of Sudbury. But there is some concern whether this is a legitimate abatement technique. Supporters of the high stack claim that the effluent is dispersed and rendered harmless, with results equivalent to 90 per cent abatement (Bangay, 1973, 42). Their opponents believe that the stack merely spreads damages over a wider area. The solution to this controversy can only be determined after considerable empirical work.

Additional considerations in the determination of social abatement costs are dislocation costs. These include the social costs incurred if abatement costs caused the smelter complexes to cease operation in the Sudbury region or if it caused plant layoffs and resulting layoffs in the dependent service sector of Sudbury. The costs involved are short-term unemployed capacity and population relocation costs.

Environmental policy for the Sudbury airshed
The policy-relevant data for the sulphur dioxide problem in Sudbury can be briefly summarized. The marginal benefit function is zero up to some low

ambient concentration and increases irregularly with increasing concentration. Existing data could support some order-of-magnitude estimates of total current damages. Combining these estimates with the shape information and a dispersion model could yield rough marginal benefit figures for emission reductions. Marginal control cost data are scattered, but the cost of several scrubbing processes could be used as an upper limit on these costs, and technical progress may reduce these costs over the next decade. Higher stacks might reduce total damages, but a careful dispersion analysis combined with the benefit data would be needed to confirm this proposition.

While monitoring the rate of discharge of sulphur dioxide is not inexpensive, only two sources need to be monitored, so that if the problem warrants substantial expenditures on control the monitoring cost will be small compared to total control costs. Ambient monitoring at selected points around the smelters can be used at moderate cost to confirm emission measurements or to calibrate dispersion models.

Traditional approaches to this sort of problem would be to require construction of a stack of a specific height or to limit the rate at which pollution could be discharged into the air. The benefit function, however, does not suggest any particular emission rate or ambient concentration that clearly divides large damages from small; marginal damage appears to rise over a substantial range of concentrations, so that any emission standard or ambient standard would be set essentially arbitrarily. Thus the conventional standard approach seems poorly suited to this problem.

Because marginal benefits do not appear to be constant over a range of concentrations a simple effluent charge seems as ill suited to this problem as an effluent standard. It is possible, however, to design an effluent charge that would reflect the available benefit information without undue administrative complexity. Suppose the true marginal benefits are shown by the line MB in Figure 19, a function that could change seasonally. This could be approximated by an effluent charge, the magnitude of which depended upon ambient concentrations, in several discrete stages. An example of such a charge utilizing three stages is shown by line EC. As long as ambient concentrations (measured by some weighted average of monitoring stations) were below C_0 no charge would be levied. When concentrations were between C_0 and C_1 the charge would be based on e_1; when they were between C_1 and C_2 the charge would be based on e_2; and when concentrations were above C_2 charge e_3 would prevail.

Since the vertical axis in the figure is in dollars per ambient concentration, the dispersion model would be necessary to convert these e values to dollars per pound of sulphur emitted, a conversion that would be different for each source depending on location, stack height, and other factors. Consideration of stack

Figure 19
Marginal damage (benefit) as a function of ambient concentration

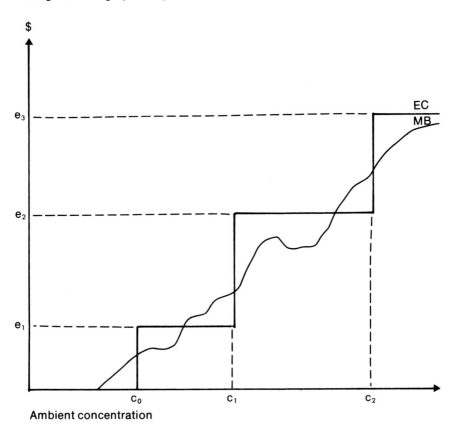

Ambient concentration

height would encourage tall stacks if that were an efficient control method. Selection of the proper effluent charge rate might be made on a weekly basis if sufficient monitoring data were available and short-run variations in benefits or emissions occurred. If important variations in damages or emission rate take place over longer periods, then monthly, seasonal or even yearly determination of the rate might be sufficient.

The advantage of basing the effluent charge on ambient concentrations is that it allows some approximation of the marginal benefit schedule in the charge itself. When the charge was first imposed, payments by the smelters would be high, justifying drastic steps to reduce emissions. As emissions and marginal damages declined, the per-unit charge would drop until some equilibrium was reached at which further abatement costs were greater than the charge. Since payments would still be substantial unless concentration C_0 had been reached there would still be an incentive to develop and adopt less expensive or more efficient abatement devices. The maximum burden on the smelters could be calculated from e_3 and the current or projected emission rate. This maximum would be the upper limit on costs to the smelters, while under a pure emission standard system no such upper limit could be calculated unless proven technology of known costs were available.

The usual reason for advocating effluent charges, that they equate marginal abatement costs among polluters, is of minor importance here since there are only two polluters. The proposed plan is superior to an emission standard, however, because it (1) internalizes the externality by raising nickel costs to include all social costs, (2) causes abatement expenditures approximating marginal benefits, (3) provides strong incentives for technical progress in pollution control, and (4) allows a flexible abatement response by the polluters.

As the population of Ontario increases the lands northeast of Sudbury become more and more valuable for tourism. The effluent charge scheme discussed above, if it does help induce technological changes as seems likely, will induce increased abatement over time, encouraging more tourism. Thus even without continuous government action gradual improvement in air quality in this region should be expected. If increased demand for recreational land raises the benefits of abatement the effluent charge schedule should also be increased, accelerating the abatement program.

AUTOMOBILE EMISSIONS IN ONTARIO

In 1972 more than 2.8 million passenger cars were registered in Ontario. This number had been growing at over 5 per cent per year, and the Systems Research Group (1970, 56) predicted 5.8 to 6.3 million automobiles registered in the province by the year 2001. These automobiles emit hydrocarbons, carbon monoxide, oxides of nitrogen, and particles of lead into the atmosphere, increasing their concentration in the ambient air, especially in large urban centers. The lead tends to fall rapidly from the air onto the soil, with most lead being removed within a few hundred feet of a highway. Carbon monoxide concentrations also decrease quite rapidly with distance from the highway since there are several natural removal processes for this pollutant. Hydrocarbons and oxides of nitrogen, however, may be transported many miles before they are dispersed, and they can combine in the presence of sunlight to form the photochemical oxidants that are the primary ingredients in smog.

While Ontario's problems are less severe than those of Los Angeles, there are occasions, particularly in the Toronto area, when photochemical smog becomes a noticeable problem. Recent studies have shown that this photochemical oxidant may be transported one hundred miles or more, so that it is frequently difficult to determine the actual origin of a high oxidant reading. Taylor (1973, 6) shows that Toronto has a population and population density within the six highest in North America. This demonstrates at least the potential for a significant automobile pollution problem originating in the greater Toronto area. Some ambient automotive pollutant concentrations are reported in Environment Canada (1974).

There is great debate about the magnitude of the harm caused by automotive air pollutants. It appears, however, that carbon monoxide may affect cognitive and psychomotor performance of motorists at some of the higher ambient concentrations now existing, although there are no known effects for most current concentrations. Lead, hydrocarbons, and oxides of nitrogen have not been proved to have adverse short-term health effects at present concentrations, but in the medical community it is feared that they may cause long-term injury and result in an increased disease rate and a reduction of life expectancy. The photochemical products of automotive emissions are unpleasant, irritating, and unhealthy at levels sometimes encountered in major urban centers. Damage to material and plant life is known to occur as a result of automobile emissions, as well as aesthetic problems such as unpleasant odour and occasionally reduced visibility.

No reliable estimates are available of total automotive pollution damage in Canada, Ontario, or Toronto. The National Academy of Sciences (1974) has estimated that the benefits from complete automobile pollution control in the United States could be between $7 and $10 billion per year. If these figures were correct and if Canadian benefits were proportional to the Canadian automobile population benefits from automobile pollution control in Ontario might be between $224 and $320 million per year; a great deal of empirical work, however, would be required to provide an accurate figure.

The costs of automobile pollution control have been recently reviewed by the National Academy of Sciences (ibid., chap. 2), which found that the cost of meeting standards for new cars increases as a function of the degree of control at any given time, but that for a given degree of control, costs decrease with time. Technological progress in automotive emission control is an important factor in determining control costs, which may reach close to $100 per year for cars meeting the final United States emission standards. An earlier set of cost estimates, presented in Dewees (1974a, chap. 7), shows other control alternatives such as testing and maintenance of used cars to be at least as expensive as the most expensive new car controls now contemplated.

The primary method of reducing automobile emissions in the past has been regulation of allowable emission rates for new cars. Table 16 shows the Canadian

TABLE 16

Canadian new car exhaust emission standards
(grams/mile)

Year	Hydro-carbons	Carbon monoxide	Nitrogen-oxide	Test
1968	3.4^a	35.0^a	NR	FTP[b]
1970	2.2	23.0	NR	FTP[b]
1972	3.4	39.0	NR	CVS-C[c]
1973	3.4	39.0	3.0	CVS-C[c]

NOTE: NR means not regulated.
a This was originally expressed as 275 ppm of
hydrocarbons and 1.5 per cent carbon monoxide.
b FTP means Federal test procedure.
c CVS-C means constant-volume sampling –
cold start only.

standards through 1974. During this time they have been identical to those
applicable in the United States. Beginning in 1975 the Canadian standards are
somewhat less strict than those in the United States, although more strict than
any previously applied in Canada. Taylor (1973) has shown that even without
the standards to be applied in 1975 the average emission rate from Canadian
automobiles would continue to decline until about 1980.

The policy alternatives open to Ontario are rather limited because of several
technological and institutional factors almost unique to this pollution source. It
seems inevitable that the best available control technology at any moment will
be that which meets the most stringent US standards. Canada has already demonstrated that if standards differ between the two countries they will be less strict
for Canada. In principle, Ontario might choose to apply the US standards rather
than the Canadian standards in the future, but because of the allocation of
powers between the federal and provincial governments this would not be easy.
Nor does Ontario have the power to adopt new car standards less strict than
those of the federal government. Thus the legal and practical constraints on the
province leave almost no power to change the emission rates for new cars sold in
the province. The only real avenue available would be to exert pressure on the
Canadian federal government to change the federal standards.

There are several other methods of affecting total automobile emissions in
the province, however. The province could establish regulations governing the
maintenance of used cars to reduce their emission rates, or reduce the rate at
which emissions increase as the car ages. The province might attempt to
reduce total motoring, which would certainly reduce total emissions. Finally,

the province might attempt to restrict automobile use in specific areas of high pollution concentration.

It was indicated above that programs for testing all vehicles on an annual basis and repairing those that do not achieve the low emissions for which they were designed have poor cost effectiveness. The cost per gram of pollution removed is at least as great as any new car program. Thus, unless Ontario felt that even the most strict United States new car standards were insufficient for Ontario, it would not make sense to adopt a comprehensive testing and maintenance program. Since Canadian opinion has tended to be that the US standards are *too* strict, comprehensive maintenance programs can be dismissed.

This does not mean, however, that nothing should be done to used cars. It seems possible that a limited program of inspection, whereby cars emitting substantial quantities of visible pollutants are tested and repairs required, might be cost effective. Since the number of such vehicles is quite small, the cost of the program would be small. Since each vehicle with highly visible emissions generally is many times dirtier than the average vehicle, repairs would probably result in a significant emission reduction. While the effect on aggregate emissions would be small, there would be a psychological gain since those whose cars were more expensive because of new car pollution controls would not feel that other cars could contribute unlimited amounts of pollution to the air.

Programs of motoring reduction may be cost effective if carried out on a limited basis. Where alternate traffic routes and transportation facilities are available it may be desirable to close portions of some downtown streets to private automobiles. This can cut automotive pollution concentrations on such streets in half, although total emissions for a metropolitan area would be unaffected since few streets could actually be closed. Reserving special lanes for exclusive bus or streetcar use has the combined effect of improving transit service and reducing highway capacity for automobiles. Both effects are likely to switch motorists into transit use. If further motoring reduction is desired the most practicable policy is to raise the price of motoring. An administratively simple means of doing this is to levy tolls upon expressways and bridges, where the tolls are sufficiently high to discourage travel noticeably. A more comprehensive but currently untried method would be to require that all automobiles submit to an odometer check once a year, and impose a tax on each vehicle proportional to the miles driven during the year. This tax might be uniform for the entire province, or higher in congested urban areas. If problems of measurement and enforcement were solved such a tax could be set at levels that would significantly reduce total motoring in a metropolitan area.

A tax of the kind just suggested could be designed more specifically to reduce aggregate emission levels. If the tax were dependent not only on the number of miles driven but also upon the emission rate of the automobile, dirty cars would be discouraged more than clean cars. It is far too expensive to measure accurately the emission rate of every car on an annual basis. The most practicable method is to determine the average emission rate for cars of each make and model for each model year. The tax would then be based, not on the individual vehicle emissions, but on the average for cars of its type, and would tend to cause retirement of high emission vehicles or to reduce their use in favour of lower-emission cars.

It is frequently suggested that subsidizing or expanding transit service will attract motorists from the highways. The empirical evidence, however, suggests that this is not the case. The existence of an efficient transit system is a prerequisite to shifting motorists to transit, but unless other policies are undertaken to make motoring less attractive, few cars are actually removed from the road. Dewees (1974b) has argued that the primary effect of many transit improvements has been to encourage people to live further from their work places.

How many of these policies should be adopted and their severity will depend upon the perception in Ontario of the auto pollution problem. If the reductions in emissions arising from new car controls reduce the problem to minimal proportions, perhaps nothing else is necessary. If in some areas the problem is still regarded as important, any or all of the above policies might be adopted.

Furthermore, if the problem is deemed to be an important one, then it is necessary to know how emissions and air quality are changing. A regular program of surveillance, in which cars are selected at random from the highways and tested for emission rates, would be vital to determining whether the new car controls were having the desired effect. An intensive monitoring program in problem areas could be used to determine whether ambient concentrations were responding to new car emission rate reductions as dispersion models predict. In a problem as complex as this, such monitoring and feedback is vital.

Bibliography

Air Pollution Working Group (1974a) 'Abnormal lead distributions and effects on the human population. Report 1: Canada Metal.' Institute of Environmental Sciences and Engineering, University of Toronto
- (1974b) 'Abnormal lead distributions and effects on the human population. Report 2: Toronto Refiners and Smelters.' Institute of Environmental Sciences and Engineering, University of Toronto
Anderson, R.J. (1970) 'Applications of engineering analysis of products to econometric models of the firm.' *American Economic Review Papers and Proceedings* 60, 398-402
Anderson, R.J. and T.D. Crocker (1971a) 'Air pollution and residential property values.' *Urban Studies* 8, 171-80
- (1971b) 'The economics of air pollution: a literature assessment.' In P.B. Downing, ed., *Air Pollution and the Social Sciences* (New York: Praeger)
Argenbright, L.P. and B. Preble (1970) 'SO_2 from smelters: three processes form an overview of recovery costs.' *Environmental Science and Technology* 4, 554-61
Arrow, K.J. (1965) 'Criteria for social investment.' *Water Resources Research* 1, 1-8
Auld, D.A. (1974) 'Willingness to pay for pollution abatement: a case study.' *Alternatives* 4, 34-6
Bangay, C. (1973) 'The dragon's breath.' *Alternatives* 2, 37-47
Barrett, Larry B. and Thomas E. Waddell (1973) *Cost of Air Pollution Damage: A Status Report for US Environmental Protection Agency.* (North Carolina: National Environmental Research Centre)

Bates, David V. (1967) 'Health costs of diseases related to air pollution.' *Pollution and Our Environment.* Vol. I (Montreal: Canadian Council of Resource Ministers)

– (1972) 'Estimate of the cost of sickness attributable to air pollution in Canada.' In *Cleaner Air: Cost-Benefits* (Ste. Adele, Quebec: Air Pollution Control Association)

Baumol, William J. (1971) *Environmental Protection, International Spillovers and Trade.* Wicksell Lectures. (Stockholm: Almquist and Wicksell)

– (1972) 'On taxation and the control of externalities.' *American Economic Review* 62, 307-22

Baumol, W.J. and W. Oates (1971) 'The use of standards and prices for protection of the environment.' *Swedish Journal of Economics* 73, 42-55

Beeton, Alfred M. (1973) 'Man's effects on the Great Lakes.' In Charles R. Goldman, James McEvoy III, and Peter J. Richerson, eds, *Environmental Quality and Water Development* 250-80 (San Francisco: W.H. Freeman)

Benson, J.R. and M. Corn (1974) 'Costs of air cleaning with electrostatic precipitators at TVA steam power plants.' *Journal of the Air Pollution Control Association* 24, 339-48

Bini, Giuseppe (1973) 'Lead in the urban environment.' *Environmental Studies* 5, 132-5

Bird, R. and L. Waverman (1972) 'Some fiscal aspects of controlling industrial water pollution.' In D.A.L. Auld, ed., *Economic Thinking & Pollution Problems* 75-102 (Toronto: University of Toronto Press)

Botts, W.V. and R.D. Oldenkamp (1973) 'The molten carbonate process for SO_2 removal from stack gases: process description, economics, and pilot plant design.' *Journal of the Air Pollution Control Association* 23, 190-3

Bradley, R.M. and P.C.G. Isaac (1969) 'The cost of sewage treatment.' *Water Pollution Control* 68, 368-402

Bramhall, D.F. and E.S. Mills (1966) 'Alternative methods of improving stream quality: an economic and policy analysis.' *Water Resources Research* 2, 355-63

Brandt, D.L. and A.N. Mann (1973) 'Preliminary estimation of costs for air and water pollution control.' *1973 Transactions of the American Association of Cost Engineers* (St Louis)

Camin, K.Q. (1969) 'Alternatives for industrial treatment.' *Water and Sewage Works* 116, IW/8-IW/13

Canadian Lead Industries Association (1974) 'Submission to the Government of Ontario on The Control of Industrial Lead Pollution.'

Carpenter, S.B., J.M. Leavitt, and W.C. Colbaugh (1970) 'Principal plume dispersion models of TVA power plants.' Paper presented at the 63rd annual meeting of the Air Pollution Control Association (St Louis)

Cesario, F.J. and J.L. Knetsch (1970) 'Time bias in recreation benefit estimates.' *Water Resources Research* 6, 700-4

Clawson, Marion and Knetsch, Jack L. (1966) *Economics of Outdoor Recreation* (Baltimore: Johns Hopkins Press for Resources for the Future Inc.)

Coase, R. (1960) 'The problem of social cost.' *Journal of Law and Economics* 3, 1-44

Coutant, C.C. (1971) 'Great Lakes ecology.' In F.A. Butrico, C.J. Touhill and C.L. Whitman, eds, *Resource Management in the Great Lakes Basin* 93-123 (Lexington, Mass.: D.C. Heath)

Crocker, T.D. (1969) 'The measurement of economic losses from uncompensated externalities.' In W.R. Walker, ed., *Economics of Air and Water Pollution* 227-47 (Blacksburg, Virginia: Virginia Water Resources Research Centre)

Dales, J. (1968) *Pollution, Property and Prices* (Toronto: University of Toronto Press)

Davidson, Paul (1967) 'The valuation of public goods.' In Morris E. Garnsey and James R. Hibbs, eds, *Social Sciences and the Environment* 125-54 (Boulder: University of Colorado Press)

Davidson, Paul, F. Gerard Adams, and Joseph Seneca (1966) 'The social value of water recreational facilities resulting from an improvement in water quality: the Delaware estuary.' In Allen V. Kneese and Stephen C. Smith, eds, *Water Research* 175-211 (Baltimore: Johns Hopkins Press for Resources for the Future Inc.)

Dennis, R. and R.H. Bernstein (1968) *Engineering Study of Removal of Sulphur Oxides from Stack Gases; Final Report* (Bedford Mass.: GCA Corporation)

Dewees, D. (1973) 'Costly information and the choice of policies for reducing externalities.' Institute of Environmental Sciences and Engineering, Pub. No. EF-10

– (1974a) *Economics and Public Policy: The Automobile Pollution Case* (Cambridge: MIT Press)

– (1974b) 'The effect of transit on driving and land use.' University of Toronto, IQASEP Policy Paper No. 11

– (1974c) 'Costs of automobile emission control standards.' In Committee on Costs and Benefits of Automobile Pollution Controls, Report to the National Academy of Sciences

Dewees, D. and W. Sims (1975) 'The symmetry of effluent charges and subsidies for pollution control.' Institute for Environmental Studies, Pub. No. EF-24

Dorfman, R. and H. Jacoby (1972) 'A public decision model applied to a local pollution problem.' in R. Dorfman and N. Dorfman, eds, *Economics of the Environment* 205-49 (New York: Norton)

Downing, P.B. (1969) *The Economics of Urban Sewage Disposal* (New York: Praeger)

- (1971) *Air Pollution and the Social Sciences: Formulating and Implementing Control Programs* (New York: Praeger)

Dreisinger, B.R. and O.C. McGovern (1969) *Sulphur Dioxide Levels and Resultant Injury to Vegetation in the Sudbury Area During the 1968 Season* Ontario Department of Mines

Eckenfelder, W.W. and D.L. Ford (1969) 'Economics of wastewater treatment.' *Chemical Engineering* 76, 109-118

Ecker, J.G. and J.R. McNamara (1971) 'Geometric programing and the preliminary design of industrial waste treatment plants.' *Water Resources Research* 7, 18-22

Edminsten, N.G. (1969) 'Air pollution control cost studies.' In W.R. Walker, ed., *Economics of Air and Water Pollution* (Blacksburg, Virginia: Water Resources Center, Virginia Polytechnic Institute)

Edminsten, N.G. and F.L. Bunyard (1970) 'A systematic procedure for determining the cost of controlling particulate emissions from industrial sources.' *Journal of the Air Pollution Control Association* 20, 446-52

Effer, W.R. (1972) 'General biological effects of air pollution.' In *Environmental Protection – Air* 145-70 (Ontario Hydro)

Environment Canada (1973) Air Pollution Control Directorate. *A Nationwide Inventory of Air Pollutant Emissions, Summary of Emissions for 1970.* Technical Appraisal Report EPS 3-AP-73-1

- (1974) Air Pollution Control Directorate. *National Air Pollution Surveillance, Monthly Summary.* Surveillance Report EPS 5-AP-74-12

Erickson, D.L. (1973) 'The effect of SO_2 on vegetation in the Sudbury region.' *Alternatives* 2, 27-31

Ethridge, D. (1970) 'An economic study of the effect of municipal sewer surcharges on industrial wastes.' PHD dissertation (North Carolina State University at Raleigh)

Evenson, D.E. and G.T. Orlob (1970) 'Economics of cannery waste treatment.' *Water and Sewage Works* 117, IW/17-IW/21

Ezzati, A. (1974) 'A probabilistic cost analysis of 2-stack flue gas desulfurization systems.' *Engineering Economist* 19, 63-85

Faith, W.L. (1966) 'Economics of motor vehicle pollution control.' *Chemical Engineering Progress* 62(10), 41-3

Financial Post (1973) *Survey of Markets 1973-1974* (Toronto: Maclean-Hunter)

Frankel, R.J. (1965) *Economic Evaluation of Water Quality. An Engineering-Economic Model for Water Quality Management.* First Annual Report (Berkeley, Cal.: SERL, University of California)

- (1965) 'Water quality management: engineering-economic factors in municipal waste disposal.' *Water Resources Research* 1, 173-86

- (1969) 'Problems of meeting multiple air quality objectives for coal-fired utility boilers.' *Journal of the Air Pollution Control Association* 19, 18-23

Frankenberg, T.T. (1962) 'Air pollution from power plants and its control.' Paper presented at the National Conference on Air Pollution (Washington DC)

Freeman, A.M. (1971) 'Air pollution and property values: a methodological comment.' *Review of Economics and Statistics* 53, 415-16

- (1974) 'On estimating air pollution control benefits from land value studies.' In A.H. Haveman, A.C. Harberger, L.E. Lynn, W.A. Niskanen, R. Turvey, and R. Zeckhauser, eds, *Benefit-Cost and Policy Analysis: 1973* 277-88 (Chicago: Aldine)

Gillette, Donald G. (1969) 'Air pollution damage to commercial vegetation.' In W.R. Walker, ed., *Economics of Air and Water Pollution* 135-56 (Blacksburg, Virginia: Water Resources Research Centre)

Gordon, A.G. and E. Gorham (1963) 'Ecological aspects of air pollution from an iron-sintering plant at Wawa, Ontario.' *Canadian Journal of Botany* 41, 1063-78

Great Britain (1954) Committee on Air Pollution. *Report* (London: HMSO)

Hartle, D.G. (1974) 'Benefit-Cost Analysis Guide.' Mimeo.

Haveman, R. (1969) 'The opportunity cost of displaced private spending and the social discount rate.' *Water Resources Research* 5, 947-57

Henderson, J.M. and R.E. Quandt (1958) *Microeconomic Theory,* (New York: McGraw-Hill)

Hepting, G.H. (1964) 'Damage to forests from air pollution.' *Journal of Forestry* 62, 630-5

Hirschleifer, J. (1970) *Investment Interest and Capital* (Englewood Cliffs, NJ: Prentice-Hall)

Hirschleifer, J., J.C. Dellaven, and J.W. Milliman (1960) *Water Supply* (Chicago: University of Chicago Press)

Hodgson, T. (1970) 'Short-term effects of air pollution on mortality in New York City.' *Environmental Science and Technology* 4, 589-97

Holterman, S.E. (1972) 'Externalities and public goods.' *Economica* 39, 78-87

Holtmann, A.G. and R. Ridker (1965) 'Burial costs and premature death.' *Journal of Political Economy* 73, 284-6

Horowitz, J. (1973) 'The effectiveness and cost of retrofit for reducing automobile emissions.' *Journal of the Air Pollution Control Association* 23, 295-7 and 418

Hunter, W.D. (1973) 'Reducing SO_2 in stack gas to elemental sulphur.' *Power* 117(9), 63-5

Ingram, G. (1975a) 'Predicting urban air quality — a macroanalysis of pollution control strategies.' In F.P. Grad et al., *The Automobile and the Regulation of its Impact on the Environment* chapt. 4 (Norman, Oklahoma: University of Oklahoma Press)

– (1975b) 'Simulating the urban air pollution environment.' In F.P. Grad et al., *The Automobile and the Regulation of its Impact on the Environment* chap. 5 (Norman, Oklahoma: University of Oklahoma Press)

Johnson, E.L. (1967) 'A study in the economics of water quality management.' *Water Resources Research* 3, 291-305

Johnston, J. (1960) *Statistical Cost Analysis* (New York: McGraw-Hill)

Jones, A. Craig (1969) 'Studies to determine the costs of soiling due to air pollution: an evaluation.' In W.R. Walker, ed., *Economics of Air and Water Pollution* 146-56 (Blacksburg, Virginia: Virginia Water Resources Research Center)

Jones, J.R. Ericksen (1964) *Fish and River Pollution* (London: Butterworth)

Katell, S. (1966) 'Removing sulfur dioxide from flue gas.' *Chemical Engineering Progress* 62(10), 67-73

Katell, S. and K.D. Plants (1967) 'Here's what SO_2 removal costs.' *Hydrocarbon Processing* 46(7), 161-4

Katz, M. (1952) 'The effect of sulphur dioxide on conifers.' *Proceedings of the US Technical Conference on Air Pollution* 84

– (1937) *Effect of Sulphur Dioxide on Vegetation* (Ottawa: National Research Council of Canada)

Keelev, E., M. Spence, and R. Zeckhauser (1971) 'The optimal control of pollution.' *Journal of Economic Theory* 4, 19-34

Kerri, K.D. (1960) 'An economic approach to water quality control.' *Journal of the Water Pollution Control Federation* 38, 1883-97

Kneese, Allen V. (1967) 'Economics and the quality of the environment – some empirical experiences.' In Morris E. Garnsey and James R. Hibbs, eds, *Social Sciences and Environment* 165-93 (Boulder: University of Colorado Press)

Kneese, Allen V. and B.T. Bower, (1968) *Managing Water Quality: Economics, Technology, Institutions* (Baltimore: Johns Hopkins Press)

Kneese, A., R. Ayres, and R. D'Arge (1970) *Economics and the Environment* (Baltimore: Johns Hopkins Press)

Knetsch, Jack L. (1964) 'The influence of reservoir projects on land value.' *Journal of Farm Economics* 46, 231-43

Knetsch, Jack L. and Robert K. Davis (1966) 'Comparisons of methods for recreation evaluation.' In Allen V. Kneese and Stephen C. Smith, eds, *Water Research* 125-42 (Baltimore: Johns Hopkins Press for Resources for the Future Inc.)

Kohn, R.E. (1971) 'Optimal air quality standards.' *Econometrica* 39, 983-95

– (1970a) 'Abatement strategy and air quality standards.' In A. Atkinson and R.S. Gaines, eds, *Development of Air Quality Standards* (Riverside, Calif.: Environmental Resources Inc.)

- (1970b) 'Linear programming model for air pollution control: a pilot study of the St Louis airshed.' *Journal of the Air Pollution Control Association* 20, 78-82

Kuiper, E. (1971) *Water Resources Project Economics* (London: Butterworths)

Labour Council of Metropolitan Toronto, et al. (1974) 'Submission to the Government of Ontario on the control of industrial lead pollution.'

Lave, Lester B. (1972) 'Air pollution damage: some difficulties in estimating the value of abatement.' In A.V. Kneese and B.J. Bower, eds, *Environmental Quality Analysis: Theory and Method in Social Sciences* 213-42 (Baltimore: Johns Hopkins Press for Resources for the Future Inc.)

Lave, Lester B. and E. Seskin (1970) 'Air pollution and human health.' *Science* 169, 723-33

Linzon, Samuel N. (1958) 'The influence of smelter fumes on the growth of white pine in the Sudbury regions.' Ontario Department of Lands and Forests and Ontario Department of Mines

- (1960) 'The development of foliar symptoms and the possible cause and origin of white pine needle blight.' *Canadian Journal of Botany* 38, 153-61

- (1971) 'Economic effects of sulphur dioxide on forest growth.' *Journal of the Air Pollution Control Association* 21, 81-6

Leontief, W. (1970) 'Environmental repercussions and the economic structure: an input-output approach.' *Review of Economics and Statistics* 52, 262-71

Logan, J.A., W.D. Hatfield, G.S. Russell, and W.R. Lynn (1962) 'An analysis of the economics of wastewater treatment.' *Journal of Water Pollution Control Federation* 34, 860-82

M.W. Kellogg Co. (1972) 'Detailed cost breakdown for selected sulphur oxide control processes.' (Houston: National Technical Information Services)

McGovern, P.C. and D. Balsillie (1973) 'How sulphur dioxide affects vegetation in the Sudbury area.' *Water and Pollution Control* 3 (April), 70-9; 3 (June), 48-9

Mäler, K.G. (1971) 'A method of estimating social benefits from pollution control.' *Swedish Journal of Economics* 73, 121-33

Meade, J.E. (1952) 'External economies and diseconomies in a competitive situation.' *Economic Journal* 62, 54-67

Meadows, D.H., D.L. Meadows, J. Randers, and W. Behrens, III (1972) *The Limits to Growth* (New York: Signet)

Michelson, Irving and Boris Tourin (1966) 'Comparative method for studying costs of air pollution.' US Department of Public Health. *Public Health Reports* 81, 505-11

Mishan, E.J. (1971a) 'An evaluation of life and limb: a theoretical approach.' *Journal of Political Economy* 79, 687-705

- (1971b) 'The postwar literature on externalities: an interpretative essay.' *Journal of Economic Literature* 9, 1-28

National Academy of Sciences (1974) Coordinating Committee on Air Quality Studies. *Air Quality and Automobile Emission Control* Vol. 4, *The Costs and Benefits of Automobile Emission Control.* Senate Committee on Public Works (Washington DC: US Government Printing Office)

Nelson, F. and L. Shenfield (1965) 'Economics engineering and air pollution in the design of large chimneys.' *Journal of the Air Pollution Control Association* 15, 355-61

Nourse, H. (1967) 'The effect of air pollution on house values.' *Land Economics* 43, 181-9

O'Connor, J.J. (1913) *The Economic Cost of the Smoke Nuisance to Pittsburgh.* Smoke Investigation Bulletin No. 4. (Pittsburgh: Mellon Institute)

O'Connor, J.R. and J.F. Citarella (1970) 'An air pollution control cost study of the steam electric power generating industry.' *Journal of the Air Pollution Control Association* 20, 283-8

Ontario (1973a) Ministry of the Environment. 'A report on the expected performance of a proposed new chimney stack at Toronto Refiners and Smelters Limited, 28 Bathurst Street, Toronto'

– (1973b) Ministry of the Environment, Air Management Branch. 'Interim report on lead in the vicinity of secondary lead smelters in Metropolitan Toronto

– (1973c) Ministry of the Environment. *Guidelines and Criteria for Water Quality Management in Ontario* (Toronto)

Paehlke, R.C. (1973) 'Editorial comment.' *Alternatives* 2

Peltzman, S. and T. Tideman (1972) 'Local versus national pollution control: note.' *American Economic Review* 62, 959-63

Polinsky, A. Mitchell (1973) 'Essays in public sector economics: central and local.' *National Tax Association Proceedings* 516-19

Polinsky, A. Mitchell and Daniel L. Rubinfeld (1975) *Property Values and the Benefits of Environmental Improvements: Theory and Measurement.* Discussion Paper No. 67, Institute of Public Policy Studies, University of Michigan, Ann Arbor

Prest, A.R. and R. Turvey (1972) 'The main questions.' In R. Layard, ed., *Cost Benefit Analysis* (Middlesex, England: Penguin)

ReVelle, C.S., D.P. Loucks, and W.R. Lynn (1967) 'A management model for water quality control.' *Water Resources Research* 39, 1164-83

Ridker, R. (1967) *Economic Costs of Air Pollution* (New York: Praeger)

Ridker, R. and J. Henning (1967) 'The determinants of residential property values with special reference to air pollution.' *Review of Economics and Statistics* 49, 246-57

Roberts, M. (1974) 'The limits of *The Limits to Growth.*' In E. Erickson and L. Waverman, eds, *The Energy Question* 1 (Toronto: University of Toronto Press)

Roth, T.P. (1973) 'Classical vs process analysis and the form of the production function.' *The Engineering Economist* 19, 47-54

Rowan, P.P., K.L. Jenkins, and D.H. Howells (1961) 'Estimating sewage treatment plant operation and maintenance costs.' *Journal of the Water Pollution Control Federation* 33, (1973) 111-21

Rush, D., J.C. Russel, and R.E. Iverson (1973) 'Air pollution abatement on primary aluminium potlines: effectiveness and cost.' *Journal of the Air Pollution Control Association* 23, 98-104

Samuelson, Paul A. (1954) 'The pure theory of public expenditure.' *Review of Economics and Statistics* 36, 387-9

– (1955) 'Diagrammatic analysis of the theory of public expenditure.' *Review of Economics and Statistics* 37, 350-6

Scarth, William M. (1973) 'Discussant.' *National Tax Association Proceedings,* 523-7

Schelling, T.C. (1968) 'The life you save may be your own.' In S. Chase, ed., *Problems of Public Expenditure Analysis* 127-76 (Washington DC: Brookings Institution)

Scitovsky, T. (1954) 'Two concepts of external economics.' *Journal of Political Economy* 62, 70-82

Selzler, D.R. and W.D. Watson (1974) ' "Hot" versus "enlarged" electrostatic precipitation of fly ash: a cost-effectiveness study.' *Journal of the Air Pollution Control Association* 24, 115-21

Seneca, Joseph J. (1969) 'Water recreation, demand and supply.' *Water Resources Research* 5, 1179-85

Sims, W. and D. Amborski (1974) 'The effect of costly information on the enforcement of industrial water pollution effluent standards: a survey of jurisdictions.' Institute for Environmental Studies, Pub. No. ES-23

Slack, A.V., H.L. Falkinberry, and R.E. Harrington (1972) 'Sulphur oxide removal from waste gases: Lime-limestone scrubbing technology.' *Journal of the Air Pollution Control Association* 22, 159-66

Smith, R. (1968) 'Cost of conventional and advanced treatment of waste water.' *Journal of the Water Pollution Control Federation* 40, 1546-74

Smith, V.L. (1966) *Investment and Production* (Cambridge. Mass.: Harvard University Press)

Statistics Canada (62-002, Jan. 1975) Prices and Price Indexes (Ottawa: Information Canada)

Stein, J. (1971) 'The 1971 report of the president's council of economic advisors: micro-economic aspects of public policy.' *American Economic Review* 61, 531-7

Stevens, Joe B. (1966) 'Recreation benefits from water pollution control.' *Water Resources Research* 2, 167-82

Systems Research Group (1970) *Canada Transportation Projections to the Year 2000* (Toronto: Systems Research Group)

Taylor, G.W. (1973) 'Automobile Emission Trends in Canada 1960-1985' Environmental Impact and Assessment Report EPS 8-AP-73-1, Air Pollution Control Directorate, Environment Canada

Turvey, R. (1963) 'On divergences between social cost and private cost.' *Economica* 30, 309-13

Tihansky, D.P. (1972) 'A cost analysis of waste management in the steel industry.' *Journal of the Air Pollution Control Association* 22, 335-41

– (1974) 'Historical development of water pollution control cost functions.' *Journal of the Water Pollution Control Federation* 46, 813-33

US (1966a) Department of Health, Education and Welfare. *Estimating the Cost of Illness.* Health Economics Series No. 6. by Dorothy Rice. (Washington, DC: US Government Printing Office)

– (1966b) Public Health Service. *The Problem of Estimating Total Costs of Air Pollution, A Discussion and An Illustration* by R. Ridker (Washington, DC: US Government Printing Office)

– (1969a) Department of Health, Education and Welfare, Public Health Service, *Control Techniques for Particulate Air Pollutants* (Washington, DC: US Government Printing Office)

– (1969b) Department of Health, Education, and Welfare, National Air Pollution Control Administration. *Sulphur Oxide Removal from Power Plant Stack Gas* by the Tennessee Valley Authority. Contract No. TV-29233A (Springfield, Va.: NTIS

– (1969c) National Air Pollution Control Administration. *Air Quality Criteria for Sulfur Oxides* (Washington, DC: US Government Printing Office)

– (1971) Environmental Protection Agency (EPA) *Evaluation of SO_2 Control Processes* by M.W. Kellogg Co., Pictaway, NJ. Contract No. CPA70-68 (Springfield, Va.: NTIS)

– (1972a) Environmental Protection Agency. *Biological Aspects of Lead: An Annotated Bibliography.* Parts 1 and 2 by Irene R. Campbell and Estelle G. Mergard (Washington DC: US Government Printing Office)

– (1972b) Environmental Protection Agency. *'Health Hazards of Lead.'* (Mimeo.)

US Senate (1974) Committee on Public Works. *Air Quality and Automobile Emission Control* 4, 175-309 (Washington DC: US Government Printing Office)

Viner, J. (1931) 'Cost curves and supply curves.' *Zeit. Nationalokonomie* 3, 23-46. Reprinted in (1953) *Readings in Price Theory* (New York: Blakistan)

Vroom, A.H. (1971) *Sulphur Utilization* (Ottawa: National Research Council of Canada)

Watson, W.D. (1974) 'Costs and benefits of fly ash control.' *Journal of Economics and Business* 26, 167-81

Wilson, R.D. and D.W. Minnotte (1969) 'A cost benefit approach to air pollution control.' *Journal of the Air Pollution Control Association* 19, 303-8

Woodcock, K.R. and L.B. Barrett (1970) 'Economic indicators of the impact of air pollution control. Gray iron foundries: a case study.' *Journal of the Air Pollution Control Association* 20, 72-7

Yocom, John E. and Roy O. McCaldin (1968) 'Effects of air pollution on materials.' In Arthur C. Stern, ed., *Air Pollution* 2nd ed. 1, 617-54 (New York: Academic Press)

Young, C.R. (1959) *An Introduction to Engineering Economics* (Toronto: University of Toronto Press)

Young, G.K., T. Popowchak, and G.W. Burke (1965) 'Correlation of degree of pollution with chemical costs.' *Journal of the American Water Works Association* 57, 293-7

Zerbe, Richard O. jr (1969) 'The economics of air pollution: a cost-benefit approach.' Report to the Department of Public Health, Government of the Province of Ontario.

—